JOURNEY TO
THE ISLAND OF THE SUN

Also by Alberto Villoldo and Erik Jendresen

Four Winds: A Shaman's Odyssey into the Amazon

JOURNEY TO THE ISLAND OF THE SUN

THE RETURN TO THE LOST CITY OF GOLD

ALBERTO VILLOLDO
AND
ERIK JENDRESEN

HarperSanFrancisco
A Division of HarperCollins*Publishers*

The Four Winds Society and Dr. Alberto Villoldo are actively involved in the preservation of the traditions of the ancient Americas, and sponsor study programs introducing individuals to the cultural and ecological imperatives of the Amazon and highlands of Peru. For more information on their work please write:

The Four Winds Society
P.O. Box 97
Easthampton, MA 98920

JOURNEY TO THE ISLAND OF THE SUN: *The Return to the Lost City of Gold.* Copyright © 1992 by Alberto Villoldo and Erik Jendresen. All rights reserved. Printed in the United States of America. No part of this book may be used or reproduced in any manner whatsoever without written permission except in the case of brief quotations embodied in critical articles and reviews. For information address HarperCollins Publishers, 10 East 53rd Street New York, NY 10022.

Text design by Detta Penna

FIRST EDITION

Library of Congress Cataloging-in-Publication Data

Villoldo, Alberto
    Journey to the island of the sun : the return to the lost city of gold / Alberto Villoldo and Erik Jendresen. — 1st ed.
      p. cm.
    ISBN 0–06–0250895–4 (alk. paper)
      1. Shamanism. 2. Incas—Religion and mythology. 3. Villoldo, Alberto. I. Jendresen, Erik. II. Title
BF1622.I4V55 1992
299'.8—dc20   91–58160
                                            CIP

92 93 94 95 96 ❖ HAD 10 9 8 7 6 5 4 3 2 1

For Malcolm Dan Jendresen
and
Ian Pedro McCulloch-Villoldo,
a father and a son.

CONTENTS

PREFACE

In the spring of 1988, Dr. Alberto Villoldo returned to Peru to find the friend who had first revealed to him the legacy of the medicine men and women of ancient Peru. What had begun in 1973 as a romantic quest to experience the effects of a legendary jungle medicine had evolved into a life's work: the study and practice of ancient American shamanism. In 1988 Alberto was introducing Westerners to a contemporary form of ancient psychology, and I was writing the text of his South American adventures, *The Four Winds: A Shaman's Odyssey into the Amazon*. In that volume we attempted to articulate a model of human consciousness based on the journey of the Four Winds, an itinerary for accessing exquisite states of being. This legendary odyssey, marked by the four cardinal points of the Medicine Wheel, is a quest, a hero's journey, an adventure of mind, body, and spirit alien to those of us whose roots are in the West, whose faith is based on a reductionistic science and a theology of redemption.

And the ink was still drying on that manuscript when this volume began to write itself. Alberto returned to Peru to find Antonio Morales and once again found himself walking the treacherous and magical pathway of the "caretakers of the Earth," the first storytellers, the first psychologists. The shamans' task has always been to maintain a connection to the forces of Creation by exploring and knowing the domains of human consciousness and understanding the experiences of the senses. And they expressed their adventures in the stories that they told; they invested their society with the benefits of their visions.

At the dawn of the third millennium, we have become accustomed to traditions based on the stories of the experiences and adventures of those men and women who have made epic journeys of discovery — many of them over a thousand years ago. Today it is easy to believe that there are no new frontiers; it is convenient to accept the interpretations of the experiences of others. But the frontiers of a thousand years ago are as different from those of today as we are from the people who told the very first story. We are all of us pioneers, but few of us have taken the time or seized the opportunity to see for ourselves what lies just beyond or just behind the familiar world.

The old myths by which we have lived—the stories of ancient gods and heroes—no longer serve. Our standards and values and principles are atrophying from disuse. As we gain supremacy over our physical world, we seem to abdicate responsibility for everything else. We become glazed-eyed, slack-jawed, more concerned with making a living than making a life for ourselves, content to settle for a consensual reality and shrink-wrap standards and commercial values and selfish principles that seduce us into spending our money and, therefore, our time in order to accumulate what we can.

And after all, life is not about being a marketplace conquistador who has misinterpreted the meaning of abundance and is willing to sacrifice others for commercial gain, any more than it is about running off to the mountains and shaking rattles and beating drums and imitating Indians.

This is the story of one man's adventures in a world unfamiliar to most readers, although it is the world of our common ancestors. A story is the vessel that holds an experience, and this is a new vessel based on an ancient and simple design. The experience also is new. It happened a few years ago, and it is true.

Erik Jendresen
February 1, 1992
Sausalito, California

"I al oro asimismo decían que era lagrimas que el Sol llorava."
—*Conquista i Poblacion del Piru, MS.*   Cieza de Leon

*("And of the gold, likewise,
they said that it was the tears
shed by the Sun.")*

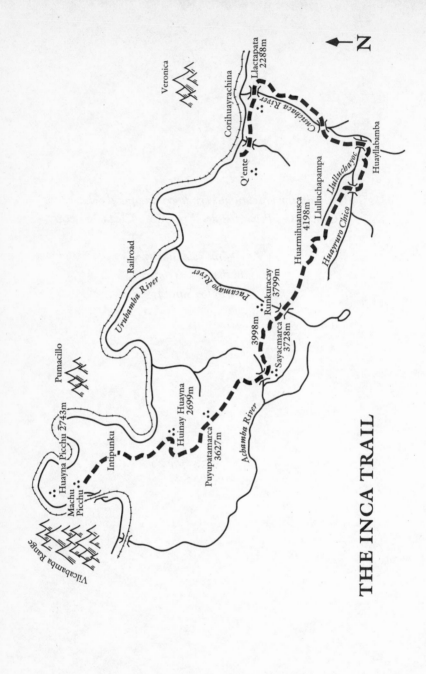

THE INCA TRAIL

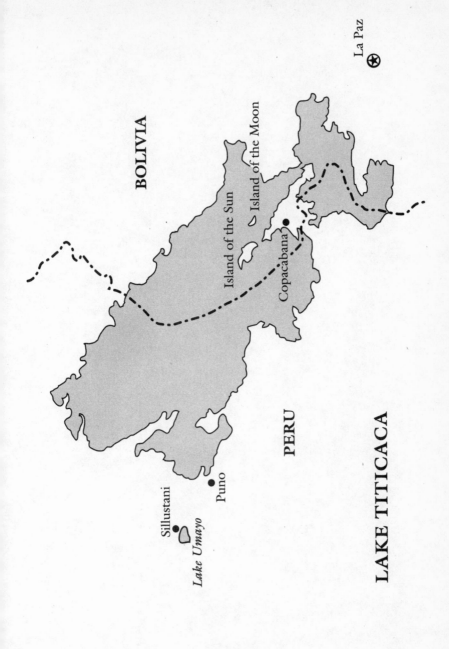

PROLOGUE

At 14,000 feet in the Andes, every step is a meditation. It must be so; otherwise you succumb to the fatigue that lurks, that waits on a moment's hesitation, a lapse of concentration, a breath out of step.

Should I falter, slacken my pace, I lose—stagger cliff-side, chest heaving, heart and lungs swollen, head swimming sickeningly, flesh sweating chillingly in the cold, thin air. But the mountain leads me, pulls me toward this morning's goal if every step is a meditation.

Every step. Two. Three.

Lift my eyes from my boots, treading the narrow Inca path; look up a thousand feet to the snow line and I can see the pass, Huarmihuañusca, Dead Woman's Pass, traces of pre-Columbian steps . . .

My path leads there, but indistinctly, a scratch in the mountainside. I shield my eyes from the too-bright white sky and look away, look at anything but that inaccessible place in the snow. Left, a steep slope rises: 1,200 feet of granite-studded terra-cotta soil and the stubble of highland grass. Right, across the valley and up: scattered ice patches in the shadow of the peak. Down, nothing to stop me should I stumble to the yellow-green pasture, where a condor is soaring above the edge of the valley forest, a jungle of vines, rotting leaves, and orange lichen.

I can hear him coming . . .

Behind the beating of my heart, another sound, a constant, bouncing, shifting sound: his pack jostling, a backpack riding bareback, rising and falling with every springing step. Does he breathe? A chilling thought.

He will not see me like this. I will stop.

Here, shrug off my pack, fall back against the jagged rock incline. A warm ache stiffens my legs and I stretch them out before me. The pain will pass quickly and inertia will set in. A body at rest tends to remain at rest.

1

Down along the way I have come I see the rock I remember passing when I noticed the condor.

I cannot see him, but he is coming. I can hear his boots scraping on the ancient paving stones. I bend to my right and remove my journal from a zipper compartment. The binding is warped from this morning's dew and the pages are all wavy. With a pencil I write:

> I cannot see him, but he is coming. Fast now, up the path behind me. He shall not reach the pass before me. I am sure, somehow, that it would satisfy his perverse sense of play, and I won't have it, won't have him looking down at me from that height.
>
> Machu Picchu is two days away.

The pencil point lingers on the period. My heart has slowed to its old rhythm and my breathing is regular, deep lungsful of crisp air. I am alone in a high Andean valley on a footpath of half-buried interlocking blocks of stone laid down by the Children of the Sun centuries ago. I hear nothing now but the whisper of the wind over the wings of the condor in the valley far below.

January 4, 1988
San Francisco

A new year, and I have begun a new journey in my sleep, or . . . where dreams play. Write them down or the memory vanishes, wisps away like the shape of a cloud in the sky. Last night's dream resonates uncomfortably and leads me to wonder if I have not dreamt it before.

In the dream I was hiking an impossible trail along the left side of a steep Andean valley, struggling toward a pass between two summits. Out of shape, out of breath, out of my element, but I knew the place the way you know things in a dream.

I knew that I had passed through a jungle, the entrance to the valley, followed a stream to a small level pasture where the walls of the valley rose dramatically. I followed an ancient path along the mountainside and up toward the pass. I knew the name of the pass . . .

As if all of this were not too vivid, too ripe for classical analysis, someone was following me, or I was following him. I am confused by this point, and this is what reminds me of the first dream. He dogs my footsteps, yet somehow taunts me to follow *him*.

I even remember stopping to catch my breath and to wait for him, and writing about it here, in my journal.

Machu Picchu was two days away.

I never saw his face.

I follow and I pursue. In either case I proceed, to return to a place that I have been, by a road that I have never traveled, with a companion that I never see.

PART I

THE FIRST STORY
EVER TOLD

1

*I am always at a loss to know how much
to believe of my own stories.*

—*Washington Irving*

"NOW, WHERE WAS I?"

A voice said: "At the beginning."

"The first story ever told," said another.

A circle of faces hovered, sun-colored masks around the campfire. Bodies were bunched together, wrapped in sleeping bags and ponchos, huddled against the cold.

I looked up, squinting against the fire's glare, to the canyon rim two hundred feet above us. The rim was discernible only as the place in the blackness where the stars began; a pin-pricked black canopy stretched from rim to rim. The moon had crossed this way hours ago, and we had built the fire by the silver-gray light that had filled Canyon de Chelly. Now there were only stars, brightly shining in the chill night air, a fire burning on the floor of the box canyon.

We had flown into Albuquerque yesterday, January 15, 1988, a group of twelve. Three were psychologists; there was a medical doctor, two attorneys, a painter, an architect, a physicist, a musician, a dance therapist, and someone who worked for the Defense Department. All were friends. We had met in the summer and the fall, in Grand Canyon and Death Valley. Yesterday we had driven to the northeast corner of Arizona and hiked two hours into Canyon de Chelly. This morning we had trekked for four hours along the canyon floor to the Anasazi cliff dwellings; then six hours to the box canyon, where we would engage in what the first inhabitants of this place would call the realm of mastery and ancient knowledge, the most esoteric of the four directions of an ancient Medicine Wheel. We were in Hopi land. Although it is a Navajo reservation, Canyon de Chelly is the birthplace of the Anasazi: the "first people," the "ancient ones," ancestors of the Hopi, one of the lost tribes of the Americas.

I struck a match, held it above the tobacco pressed into the bowl of a pipe, then drew deeply and the flame was sucked into the tobacco and the flavor was sucked into my lungs. I exhaled and watched the breath cloud dissipate, torn to shreds by the warm air rising from a fire that crackled, sparked, and hissed just as it was supposed to. I tamped the tobacco, pressed it into the bowl, relit it, and passed it to my left.

"The first story ever told," I said, "was told to me by the light of a fire. The best light to write by, to make love by, to tell stories by. It was told to me by a shaman. In Peru. Many years ago."

I closed my eyes and let the firelight penetrate my eyelids, waver red-orange. I listened to the hiss and crackle, leaned forward from the waist and felt the fire buffet my face, redden my cheeks. For an instant I knew that I could have opened my eyes and seen Antonio, Professor Antonio Morales, sitting across from me, his legs curled up under his poncho, his hat and stick and little pouch beside him on the dirt. Tuned to the moment and the pulse of this place, time and space flexible, I knew that I could lose my immediate purpose and speak with him across the years and the thousands of miles that separated us. The opportunity surprised me. It always has. I have become accustomed to being surprised.

I acknowledged my old *compadre*'s presence, and grinning, brought myself back to my present purpose. I opened my eyes and smiled at the faces drawn closer to the fire. My voice was just above a whisper when I said: "You remember this story." I looked into the eyes of my friends around the circle. "Don't you? The first story? Of course you do. Remember? It began when the Sun shed a tear."

The pipe had completed its circuit. A white hand protruding from a black sweater held it before me. I took it with both hands and nodded. I drew its smoke into my mouth and blew it down the front of my parka.

"Time was young when the Sun shed a tear that fell upon the Earth. The Earth was a maiden and the Sun was the brightest star in the heavens. And the Earth courted the Sun, orbiting the object of its love, turning to show off her every aspect, spinning round, like a young girl pirouetting, seducing the Great Star with her blue-green beauty, while Sister Moon circled in attendance, *la comadrona,* the chaperon." I passed the pipe to my left. It was good for one more circuit.

"Now the truth is that the Sun had always favored the Earth, but there was a time when the Great Star's attentions had been taken by the Moon for her own. But the light of the Sun *always* shone upon the Earth, for it was the true object of his passion. The Old Maid Moon resigned herself to their love, and although she was devoted to the Earth and would attend her faithfully, she found that she could not look steadily upon the lovers, and took to hiding her sadness in shadow.

"And it was at such a time, when the face of the Moon was hidden behind a shadow shroud, that the Sun and the Earth, free from the attentions of their pale matron, consummated their love."

I drew a deep breath, grinned, nodded a couple of times. The story sounded well. The words were forming themselves. The faces were smiling, closer to the fire, where the words rose on the warm air.

"Of course, the Earth was pregnant with life for quite some time. And the seas became swollen with child, for life grew in the Earth's ocean womb. And Sister Moon, faithful matron, became midwife, for everybody knows that the seas respond to her.

"Then one day the Sun smiled, the Moon beamed, the Earth sighed, and life was born.

"And the Sun shed a tear of joy that landed on the Earth." I tossed a length of wood into the fire. The older embers crumbled and sent a spray of sparks into the air.

"Remember?" The pipe passed to me. The bowl was cool and I tapped it on the heel of my hand and it coughed out a little ash cloud. "It fell in the land of the Stone People," I said. "A tear of fire."

A voice said: "The Stone People?"

Another said: "The Stone People. The first to tell this story."

"That's how we remember it," I said. "The Stone People told us." I turned my head and felt the faces move with mine, peer into the darkness to the rock face behind me, follow my gaze around the contours of the canyon walls that surrounded us, contained us.

"You see, before the plants and the animals there were the Stone People," I said. "And as life emerged from the ocean womb, the Stone People gathered around the tear of fire that the Sun had shed, and they wondered what to do."

A voice said: "They formed a circle around the fire and as long as the circle was unbroken, the fire stayed within and burned, and there was warmth and light even when the Sun was shining on another part of the Earth."

"The only problem," I said, "was what to do with this great tear of fire. Remember?"

I watched the faces, surveyed their eyes. Some were fixed on the fire, trance-like; some were cast down, intimidated or trying too hard to come up with something to add to the story.

"They came from everywhere, the Stone People did," said a voice to my left.

"Even from the sea," said another.

"They moved real slow," said the first.

"That's right," I said. "And the smooth Sea Stones dried before this fire, felt the moisture leave them, turn to mist, and the Stone People knew that this was a magical thing, to be cared for. But how?" Silence.

I waited, watched the faces staring at the fire or down at the circle of stones; I waited while the fire crackled, sparked, and hissed, then: "They were confounded," said a voice so clear that it cut through the night. "Those who had formed the first circle had long since been relieved by others, and they knew that they must find a place for this gift or remain there in council around the fire, its caretakers forever. And the Moon would show her face full many times, and the Earth would dance around and around the Sun while the Stone People sat in council and deliberated what to do. And the debate was long because every word they spoke took them one full year to pronounce."

"You see," I said, after a moment's pause, "you do remember." But in that instant I recognized that it was my voice that had cut through the night. I had just failed to realize it at the time. It was working: The words were not mine, although they had formed on my lips. I shivered involuntarily, took a deep breath, and prayed that the phenomenon would settle on the rest of the group. I closed my eyes and picked up the thread.

"You remember that the Stone People did not measure time, and that all this while life was growing on the shores of the Earth. It had emerged from the sea womb and nestled against the breast of the Earth and still the fire burned in the center of an ever-growing circle of Stone People. There were those who told of a great cavern in the center of the Earth, the place of their origins. All agreed that this would be an appropriate place for this shimmering tear, but the only problem was how to take it there."

I checked the faces again. By now many were nodding, staring into the fire, and nodding, smiling. The mood was lightening. I threw another branch on the fire. "What happened?" said a voice.

"Remember," said another.

"Close your eyes and remember," I said. We are in the place of the ancestors, the home of the Anasazi, those whom the Hopi called 'the first people.' The answers are here. Find them. Find them by remembering. It is very easy."

I closed my eyes and breathed the air of the place, let my mind wander.

"The circle couldn't hold," said a voice. "Could it?"

"The ground trembled with their agitation," answered another. "But the Stone People could no longer contain the object of their wonder, and the tear of fire spread to the four directions."

There was a long pause. "It sought the crevices," I said. "It filled the cracks in the rocks, and fell into the deep ravines, and followed the great underground streams all the way to the center of the Earth, where it will burn forever."

I opened my eyes and saw the smiles. I touched the ground and looked up to the rim of the canyon. "Here," I said. "It happened here.

"And that is how fire came to the Earth. It was not stolen from the Gods, as many of our myths would have us believe. It was a gift, a proud father's tear of joy."

I brought my hands together and leaned over them, automatically acknowledging the moment. "And that is why the Moon hides her face, how the Sun's passion burns deep within the heart of the Earth. It is why we build a circle of stones to contain our fires. And it is why some stones, stones that remember, have the power of the Sun within them. Whenever they put their heads together and remember the story, their memory is a spark of that tear, that old flame. A spark that would be used by man to release the light of the Sun from the branches of a tree when we build a fire. But that is another part of the story," I said.

We all looked at one another then. We smiled. We had heard the first story, told the first myth, participated somehow in giving form to a memory.

So we told a story around a campfire—or, rather, a story told itself, and the setting was as dramatic as the story was simple. A shadow-black box canyon, a hole in the Earth, a fire in the center, twelve gathered around one element to save us from the cold of another, a tribe carried along on the wave of a thought, a creation myth told without effort; for the brain of effort was silenced, and we were free to listen to the music of this place, and possibly to articulate a memory.

Tomorrow I would tell them the last part, that the first story ever told was made up. It had to be. Every time it is told is the first time. And it is, of course, true. But tonight the important thing was that we remembered something, recreated the circumstances of creation, and opened our imaginations.

I sat by the remains of the fire after the others had crawled into their tents. I felt uneasy as I hunkered down, drawing my down jacket closer to me. That afternoon one of the group had hustled back to where I was bringing up the rear of our procession through the canyon. He had scuffed something with his boot, something that turned out to be a human skull. We had stood there with the hot afternoon sun reflecting off the russet canyon walls, stood there like Hamlet and Horatio entranced by the soil-stained cracked cranium in our hands.

We had not taken the time to philosophize over it, to speculate on the brain it had contained or the personality of its owner, but returned it hastily and with a prayer to the place where he had kicked it up. We were stepping on sacred ground, and I recalled something Antonio had said when I last saw him in the echo room behind the Main Temple in the ruins of Machu Picchu. "Stand on our shoulders so that you may see the distant horizon," he had said, just before walking out into the sunshine. He had added something about meeting again, then slung his bag over his shoulder and disappeared from my life. *Stand on our shoulders,* the shoulders of the ancients. Here, they were scarcely an inch below the dried clay soil.

And someone had been watching us this night. I saw his outline on the canyon rim above our fire, saw him move against the stars. Probably our guide, or his brother.

We had been led to the entrance of the canyon by a young Navajo, a professional guide. His brother, he said, would meet us with his truck at the box canyon in the morning to carry out our gear. So it was probably this brother checking on us. But the explanation did not satisfy me. I had felt presences ever since we entered the long canyon, more than the formidable potency of this remote and sacred place. It felt as if we were being watched.

I left the lingering warmth of the fire for the cold lining of my sleeping bag. I lay still, willing the eiderdown filling to insulate me from the night air, staring at the darkness.

I woke up in Peru.

Rolled over on my side, uncomfortable, disoriented. I scrambled to my knees and shut my eyes against the dizziness of waking, rising too fast, the altitude. A sharp stone cut into my knee, and I shifted awkwardly to one side. As my head cleared, I could focus on the tufts of highland grass on this saddle-shaped clearing between the snow white twin peaks of the pass. Huarmihuañusca, Dead Woman's Pass. I stood. I leaned forward and pushed myself up with my hands, turned, and looked back down into the valley.

And I remembered the final, torturous hundred yards of the ascent, remembered throwing off my pack at the summit, dropping to my knees, rolling over onto my back, and closing my eyes and willing my heart to a reasonable rate.

And I remembered falling asleep in Canyon de Chelly.

Am I in the Andes, dreaming of falling asleep in Arizona? Or in Arizona, dreaming about the Andes—

No, I told myself. *This* is the dream.

No matter. Refreshed, I turn and walk to the far side of the pass and stare down to where a river falls two hundred feet and runs along the valley floor, vanishing in a tangle of dense jungle. There are ruins across the valley, clinging to the hillside where the trail leads. Higher up, near the next pass, two small lakes; and beyond, a broad band of cirrus clouds glow pastel pink and orange in the late afternoon sky.

There is no sign of my pursuer. I am alone, 14,000 feet above the sea. But ahead, down there, on the floor of the valley, in a clearing near the bank of the little river by the edge of the jungle, there is a bright blue speck. I turn in a panic to where I dropped my pack, and my tent is gone. There are the limp webbed nylon straps that cinched it to the frame . . . I run back to the cliff edge—to the edge of the top step of the Inca path that leads down the mountainside. I scream and my voice breaks and the high-pitched echo mocks me from the other side of the valley.

In the side pouch of my pack, my journal. It falls open to the letter stuck between pages. The letter that brought me here?

I was the first one up in the morning. It was bitter cold, an hour before the sun would fill the box canyon. I built a fire for tea and coffee, and took advantage of my few moments alone to squat beside the fire and commit the night to my journal.

Another dream.

I have made the pass, only to find that my relentless companion has overtaken me while I slept. He is waiting for me at the bottom of the next valley, where he has pitched my tent.

And there was a letter. In the dream I do not remember receiving it or who sent it, but I know that it brought me there and that I should respond to this. Is it Antonio? Is my old friend and mentor pursuing me in my dreams? Taunting me? The letter. An invitation to communicate? How prosaic.

I feel scrutinized. Even in my dreams.

Here, it is the Indians. We're an odd bunch, these white folks working with all-but-forgotten traditions in the land of a people who trace their lineage back to a desert-dwelling tribe, whose relationship with their environment was legendary—a people of exemplary spirituality who worshiped the Sun and vanished eight hundred years ago without a trace.

And what is our heritage? the lineage of the colonial European? It took us no time at all to give the object of our worship a face, endow *Him* with human qualities.

How much easier it is to see the face of the Sun in a flower than it is to see the face of a Michelangelean God.

And did not the face of God infect us? After all, if God looked like a man, could not man have the qualities and values of a God? Could he not manipulate the innocent just as our Greek, Roman, and Judeo-Christian myths taught us the Gods manipulated man?

Is it any wonder that Westerners banished the Indian from the forests and fertile plains, just as Yahweh banished the Westerner from Eden?

Within the hour we were all up, tents struck, gear packed, and it was scarcely fifteen minutes later that the truck arrived. We heard it before we saw it, rounding a boulder at the entrance to the box canyon. It was a '59 Ford pickup, black and battered, and the wipers had left twin arcs in the red dust on the windshield. The driver's side door creaked open and three men slid over and climbed out. The first one, the driver, was a hulking figure dressed in black, a silver belt buckle and silver-tipped size thirteen boots. He pushed a cowboy hat back on his head and grinned.

"Howya doin'?" he said.

I said fine, and shook his hand, and smiled at his companions: an intense-looking young man with a red bandanna around his head; and an elder, a short, withered Navajo with a gray-white ponytail, wrinkled cheeks, and stoic gray eyes. The old man wore a straw cowboy hat with a curled-up brim and a crook in the front that made it look like an eagle's beak.

"All set?" asked the driver.

"What are you doing here, man?" said the young one, the one with the bandanna. He frowned and the old man studied my face.

"Forget it," said the man in black. "Let's load her up."

"We'd like to know," said the young man, and I wondered if he spoke for the old one.

I looked him in the eye and said: "We came here to camp, to visit with our ancestors."

He held my gaze for several seconds, then spat on the ground near my feet. "Not *your* ancestors, man."

"Look," I said. "There are common roots—"

"The roots are all dried up," he said.

Larry, the one who had found the skull the day before, must have sensed something in the body language of our little tableau by the truck. He drew up, beside me and to the left. Then the old man stepped forward. His face was a clean slate; it showed no emotion as he stepped in front of his young companion and touched the medicine bag that hung around my neck. It is a small, woven leather bag bunched together with a leather thong, and it bears the emblem of a rainbow arcing over the Sun. A friend in Tucson had given it to me for my birthday, and I had grabbed it impulsively from the doorknob of my clothes closet when I left San Francisco. Now the old Indian was touching it. He looked up at me, and his eyes drew mine down to the third button of his plaid shirt. His hand slid inside, next to his chest, and reemerged with an identical bag hanging on its thong.

"What do you carry?" he asked.

I reached up and pried open my little pouch and withdrew the owl, the tiny gold Inca owl that Antonio had given me the last time I saw him. I put it in the old man's hand and he rolled it around on his palm, but never took his eyes from mine. He handed it back without looking at it. He frowned, then squinted up at me and raised his brows.

"Owl Medicine," he said.

"It's from Peru," I said.

He stared at me for a moment. Then, conversationally, as though he had seen a ticket to Lima in my shirt pocket, he said: "You are going back there?"

I said yes. And it occurred to me in that moment that I had no choice, that I would respond to the letter in my dream.

He reached up with both hands and pulled at the drawstring that sealed his bag, and withdrew a delicate green twig, a sprig of sage.

"For protection," he said.

I put it with the owl back into my pouch.

"Have a nice trip," he said.

"Thanks," I said.

The driver was beaming now, relieved that the crisis had passed, enjoying the exchange, eager to pack up and head out.

The old Indian turned to the other and said: "Our traditions are our own, but our ancestors are their ancestors. We are all under the wings of the great spirit."

The young man with the bandanna looked at the ground. He was still angry but he swallowed it, clearly deferring to the old man.

"We welcome any people who come with respect," said the old Indian, and walked off to where the gear was piled.

2

Should you ask me, whence these stories?
Whence these legends and traditions?

—*Henry Wadsworth Longfellow*

THREE MONTHS LATER I FLEW TO CUZCO. LIKE A man who turns back to sleep to recover the specter of a notion left in a dream, I returned to Peru.

It was late spring in San Francisco and it would be early winter in Peru, so I packed accordingly. Clothes chosen to be worn or shed in layers were stuffed into an old frame backpack and a small, soft leather duffel bag. I even strapped my tent to the bottom of the backpack. The journal in which I had recorded my recent dreams and my work in Canyon de Chelly went with me. So did an expectation: that I would find Antonio there in Cuzco, see the friend who had first revealed to me the legends of his people, who had described an ancient pathway, shown me how to walk, and provoked me along the way.

And there was something else: a letter in an engraved envelope, tucked away with my passport in the side of my pack. It had arrived a few weeks after my return from Canyon de Chelly. An archaeologist friend, a Peruvian with close government ties, had invited me to visit the tomb of the Lord of Sipan, the warrior priest whose burial chamber had been discovered by *huaqueros*—grave robbers—near Cajamarca, on the east coast of Peru. It

18

was the richest excavated tomb in the New World, and the dig would eventually reveal layers—temple upon temple dating from A.D. 100 to 300. I would be among the first North Americans allowed to visit the site.

An old woman, a one-eyed black soothsayer whose craft I studied as a philosophy student at the University of Puerto Rico, once told me that there are those who are dreamt and those who are dreamers. I have now come to understand fully what she meant; I have lived the experience that is the source of that quaint aphorism. Or perhaps I should say that the experience lived through me. I know now what it is to dream, for I have begun to learn the lessons that lay ahead of me on the April day when I boarded the jet bound for Peru.

My mind's eye, trained to see with a brand of awareness altogether different from that of its physical twins, looks back on that spring departure and winks at the intuitive impulse that carried me back to the land of the Incas. It recognizes the recurrent dreams and the assertion of the old Hopi as subtle indications of what was to come. Through this eye I see myself sitting wide-eyed and erect for most of the all-night flight to Lima, feel my impatience and anxiety as I hurried to meet some vague expectation. After all, could anything live up to the quality of my earlier adventures?

That question, and the notion that I had made a rash decision— that I was making this solo journey in an effort to recapture something from my past—nagged at my stomach as a sort of visceral anxiety.

I touched down in Lima, as I had so many times in the last few years. My friend met me at customs, flashed an I.D. card at the customs inspectors, and they waved me through.

We were an hour into the small talk and the Lima traffic when he told me about the recent looting of the excavation site. For the next few weeks at least, the air force—in charge of security in the northern region surrounding the tomb of the Lord of Sipan—had prohibited entrance to the site.

"I am sorry," he said, "but I do have something to show you."

I contained my disappointment for another twenty minutes bumper to bumper, then we ducked into the elegant residential district of Miraflores.

My friend took me to a townhouse and up a flight of stairs to his gleaming, scrupulously decorated living room, and displayed his treasures. Gold, all of it. Exquisite ornaments, fetishes, vessels, a breastplate, regal statues of solid gold sixteen inches high, a life-sized mask like the Sun. It was simply the most magnificent collection of pre-Columbian artistry that I will ever see.

"What is this doing here?" I asked, dumbfounded by the display.

Then the door opened and a man walked in. He looked as if he had been forty days in the wilderness and had just hosed off three days ago. He wore a starched white shirt, black trousers, and *huaraches*. His hair was pomaded, slicked back from a sunburned forehead over bleached eyes. He hadn't bothered to shave. We were introduced, then he backed off to a corner. My friend dropped his voice and explained that this man was a *huaquero* and I was the excuse—the doctor from California—to view his looted goods. He wanted ten to forty thousand dollars each for pieces that would fetch a hundred to two hundred thousand at auction at Sotheby's. I played the part, tried to coax the man into revealing the rest of his plunder, but this apparently was the lot.

Eventually I made my excuses, feigned another appointment, and called for a taxi. At the door my friend thanked me, and apologized again for the problem on site.

"What are you going to do?" I asked.

He shrugged. "Buying them, or finding somebody to buy them, might be the only way of saving the pieces, keeping them together. We will see, won't we?"

So what had been an excuse for me to follow my intuition and return to Peru was over and done with, and I had only been in the country for four hours. I took the taxi back to the airport.

What was I doing here? What if Antonio was not in Cuzco? I had not heard from him in years. I knew that he had abandoned his professorship at the Universidad Nacional. He had gone back to his people to practice that which he had mastered. Even Hilda, the matronly Indian woman whose children I had "adopted" and who corresponded with me regularly, had not heard from or of him for many years.

The anxiety was turning my stomach as I walked to the AeroPeru counter and checked the departure time of the next flight to Cuzco. The plane would be delayed indefinitely due to *la garúa,* the mist of coastal fog and urban smog that haunts the capital of Peru. I forced a smile and nodded good-naturedly at the apologetic young woman behind the counter. Then I headed down to the end of the terminal, walked determinedly through the door marked *Caballeros,* and unaccountably threw up.

In the early 1970s I traveled to Peru with all the earnestness and self-absorption and immodesty of a young maverick. I had been exposed to Afro-Cuban spirituality, with its drum and candle ceremonies, as a privileged child growing up in the city of Havana before the revolution. Inspired and encouraged by a pioneer in dream research, Dr. Stanley Krippner, I had sought (in the course of a masters degree in psychology) to expose myself to many of the more phenomenal healing practices of Latin America: urban healing in Mexico, and Candomblé in Brazil. I had graduated in 1972. Then, with Dr. Krippner's guidance, I designed a nontraditional doctoral program in contemporary psychology in order to study the practices of ancient psychology. I had gone to Peru in search of the fabled *ayahuasca,* the "vine of the dead," the jungle liana that was said to take one through an experience of death and back again. I had wanted to find an *ayahuascero,* a jungle shaman, a purveyor of this legendary potion. So I had flown to Cuzco en route to the Amazon jungle, and there met a man who gave me directions.

This was Professor Antonio Morales as I remember him then: a small man in a worn and baggy 1940s pin-stripe suit, straight gray hair brushed back from a high forehead the color of mahogany. His whole face, its high cheek bones and long Inca nose, might have been carved from that hardwood. His eyes, walnut irises and ebony pupils, reminded me of Rasputin. He was a Quechua Indian, the only Indian on the university faculty. He had introduced to me the fundamental concept of the shaman, the "one who has already died," the "caretaker of the Earth." He outlined for me the fourfold path of knowledge, the Medicine Wheel, the journey of the Four Winds. He cautioned me to recognize the difference between having an experience and *serving* an experience, a distinction that I would not fully appreciate till much later. And he directed me to don Ramón Silva, an alleged *ayahuascero* who lived in the Amazon jungle south of Pucallpa.

Counting myself lucky to have found a man who had, in his words, grown up with the myths and nursed on the legends of his culture, I had headed recklessly for Pucallpa and then some sixty-odd kilometers into the jungle. I found Ramón. I tasted the *ayahuasca*. In a thatched-roof hut on the banks of a small lagoon, a backwater of the Amazon, the tips of Ramón's fingers strummed a one-stringed harp, his lips sang the songs of the jungle, and fear was redefined for me forever. In what was then the most harrowing full-sensory experience of my life, my consciousness, my very awareness of myself and my environment was altered irrevocably. Even after I succeeded in discounting the trauma of my experience as a substance-induced hallucinogenic episode, I knew that things would never be the same again.

I returned to Cuzco, and old Professor Morales listened matter-of-factly, accepted my tale effortlessly, defined my experience elegantly. It was the "work of the West," he explained; I had been rash to seek an experience of this sort without the proper preparation, without the skills to serve the experience, much less understand it. The journey of the Four Winds, as he elaborated on it then, was a metaphorical journey through the four cardinal directions of the Medicine Wheel. It begins in the South, where one goes to confront and shed the past just as the serpent sheds its skin, to learn to walk with beauty on the Earth. The serpent is the archetypal symbol of this direction. The West is the path of the jaguar, where one encounters fear and death; here one acquires posture, assumes the stance of the spiritual warrior who has no enemies in this life or the next. The dragon path leads to the North, the place of the ancestors, where one has the direct and immediate experience of knowledge, meets power face-to-face. Finally there is the East, the most difficult journey that a person of knowledge undertakes. This is the eagle path—the flight to the Sun and the journey back to one's home to exercise vision and skills in the context of one's life and work.

Here was the most elegant description of the "hero's journey" I had ever heard: a distillate of all those tales of other's experiences—the very tales that we have fashioned into the myths and religions of our species. Unencumbered by miracles, anthropomorphic gods, and the embroidery of centuries of telling, interpreting, and retelling, the Medicine Wheel was an itinerary for self-discovery and transformation. There was something irresistibly primal and elemental about it, something authoritative, as if it represented one of the earliest descriptions of the phenomenon of awareness, the mechanism of consciousness.

The professor had explained that the prerequisites for engaging this process were simple: find a *hatun laika,* a master shaman. He or she would be able to discern my intent and my purpose. If I passed muster—if my intent was impeccable and my purpose pure—he or she would guide me on my journey beyond the edge of ordinary awareness.

There was one such man whom professor Morales had heard of, a shaman, a notorious *hatun laika* who was said to wander the *altiplano,* the high chaparral plateau of southern Peru. He was called don Jicaram. His name was derived from the Quechua verb *ikarar,* "to empower." If I could occupy myself for the next two weeks until the university would be in recess, the professor would be delighted to accompany me on a walking tour of the region.

I spent those next couple of weeks living and working with an urban healer and his wife on the outskirts of Cuzco; two weeks that culminated with my submission to a ritual designed to open my "inner vision." On a chilly March night the "veil" that my hosts perceived was clouding my "vision" was carved away from my forehead with my own hunting knife. I saw things that night, witnessed another form of awareness, experienced a different sort of vision, had in effect another profound experience that I struggled to deny, to discount, to reduce to the curious effect of suggestion and traumatic ritual.

Soon thereafter Professor Antonio Morales and I had set out across the Peruvian *altiplano* in search of the notorious shaman, don Jicaram.

We had walked for almost a week; and we talked. Antonio and I would walk together for many years, make similar treks in the course of our relationship, and I would come to relish those times then as much as I have exalted them since. We became friends; we became *compadres.*

It was at the end of that first week, in an adobe hut near where the *altiplano* descends 5,000 feet to the jungle lands of the Q'ero, the "long-haired ones," that I met the man whose trail we had picked up days before. I watched the man the natives called don Jicaram free the spirit of a dying missionary woman, a white woman who had been brought to the village by Indians from the jungle below. It was my companion, Professor Morales, who worked silently, methodically, to disengage the old woman's luminous body that night and into the early morning, when he stimulated my freshly opened vision to witness the instant of her death. The man I had been traveling with was the very man that I had sought.

We never spoke of that dramatic revelation, and it took me a few days to register the complete significance of this man's double life. Feared and respected in the countryside as a master healer, idolized by a handful of university students, Antonio Morales was a man of two worlds. It was like something out of a storybook. All the time that I had been seeking this *hatun laika* as a subject for my study, he had been by my side studying me.

We began our work then in earnest. With his guidance I embarked upon the journey that has no end. In some sense we have been walking together ever since; my perceptions have been changing ever since.

We traveled together to Machu Picchu, where I engaged with the work of the South for the first time, learned what it meant to confront my past and shed it according to the traditions of shamanism—mythically, cathartically, rather than psychologically. I began to learn something of the use of certain plants to facilitate the laying of new and astonishing neural pathways in my brain. And we talked: about philosophy, about the human experience, about the nature and use of myth, the origins of psychology and storytelling, and the physics of life and death.

Two years later we traveled together to witness and participate in the death of Antonio's teacher, a gentle, ancient man who died in the company of those whom he had taught for half a century.

Then I returned to the jungle, to Ramón's little hut by the lagoon. Free from my past, I met fear and death, came ultimately to understand why the shaman is referred to as "one who has already died," one who has no unfinished business in this life or the next.

Back in the States I had written an objective analysis of primitive healing traditions that drew mostly from my earliest experiences in Mexico and Brazil. I received my doctorate in psychology and returned to Peru, only to learn that Antonio had resigned the chairmanship of the department of philosophy and had disappeared from Cuzco.

Again I returned to California and began to adapt the shamanic traditions that I had studied; I began to translate the work of the Medicine

Wheel into a Western framework, a psychology of the sacred. For I had realized long ago that the journey of the Four Winds represented an ancient formula for transformation: shed the past that restrains us (particularly the myth that we were born outcasts from Paradise), confront and overcome the fears of the future and death that paralyze us, and we may live fully in the present; apply the skills learned along the way to access a sea of consciousness as vast as time itself, then find a vehicle for expressing the experience with beauty and living as a caretaker of the Earth.

I had a notion that the Medicine Wheel could be considered as a sort of neurological map for overriding the four operative programs of our primitive limbic brain: fear, feeding, fighting, and sex. Further, I imagined that the ability to override the prime directives of the most primitive part of our brain might allow us to step into a grander consciousness. Perhaps that potential is fundamental to the next quantum leap in the evolution of our species.

So I had begun to work with groups of psychologists and other health care professionals, to introduce to them this ancient formula, to lead them on journeys of the soul. It was while conducting a workshop among the ruins of Machu Picchu, seven years after missing him at the airport in Cuzco, that I had found Antonio again. He was lecturing to a group of schoolchildren, guiding them through the ruins of the City of Light that their ancestors had built.

He was dressed as he had always dressed in the country: a pair of raw cotton trousers, sandals, a simple brown poncho, and a beat-up old fedora with a satin band. He carried a walking stick, a curious acknowledgment of his advanced years—it was not long enough to lean on, it was simply a stick to walk with.

We spoke for several minutes. He told me that remembering ancient memories—the task of the North—is not simply a matter of recalling knowledge acquired by others in the short history of our species. It is stepping through the crack between the worlds and taking our place among the twice born, all those who have conquered death, done battle with the archetypes of consciousness, and mastered the forces of Nature to become persons of knowledge. "Become them and allow them to become you," he said. "Their memories will grow in you, for they are who you are becoming." He said that history trusts us with a responsibility—a *stewardship*, he called it—and we abdicate by taking refuge in the drama of our personal past. We dishonor the lineage of our people.

"Your psychology," he said, "teaches you to reconcile yourself with the past, with your mother and your father and your history. Our psychology teaches us to reconcile ourselves with the future, to craft a destiny for ourselves and become stewards of the world that we want our children to inherit."

He had gone on to speak of the East. "It is the way of the visionary," he said. "It is where we assume full responsibility for who we are becoming and influence destiny by envisioning the possible." He said that destiny is not something over which one seeks to gain control, but a person of power can influence it. "Learn to dance with it," he said. "Lead it across the dance floor of time."

And he tapped the top of his head and said that the crack between the worlds is the gap in the skull that we are born with, the fontanel that closes soon after birth.

He had always been a poet, a master of metaphor.

So, as the end of his life drew near, Antonio Morales had turned to the children; for it all begins with the children.

He took my hand then and told me that we would meet again, that there were places where he could not go alone. A remarkable statement from a man who had traveled further within the boundless realm of his own mind than any man I will ever know.

That was in the fall of 1983. And that was the last I saw of him.

Once again I returned to the United States. I resolved to document my friendship with Antonio, to describe the shamanic experience as I had experienced it.

So now, five years later, I paid off the cab from the Cuzco airport, stepped out in front of the little café across the street from the old Hotel los Marqueses on Calle Garcilaso, and expected to see Antonio waiting for me there.

After all, I knew that our work was not complete. My dreams had called me back to this place, the travel hub of all my adventures, the landscape of my waking dreams. Is it any wonder that I half-expected to see my old friend there waiting for me?

I suppose I have become accustomed to taking the extraordinary for granted. It is axiomatic that once you begin to expect the unexpected, the unexpected is redefined. Antonio was not there. I filled my lungs with thin, cool Andean air and let it out, blinked away the dizziness and forced a smile for the little girls stationed around the great oak double door to the Hotel los Marqueses.

The girls are *laneras*, sellers of alpaca—sweaters, scarves, hats, mittens, ponchos woven with yarns dyed red, blue, green, gray, yellow, and brown, earth tones, bolds and pastels, fashioned by their own hands, their mothers' and sisters'. They know me by name and I know them, and they stopped bargaining with me long ago. Now they just smile and giggle, welcome me as though I had been gone only a week, and quote me a price that would pay for a house, knowing that I always buy what I can wear and leave with more than I can carry.

Even as I stood there kidding around with them, my eyes checked the street.

"*¿Que busca, señor?*"

"Hm?" I looked down at the youngest of three sisters, Angelina. Her eyes were wide, her little mouth open in an imperfect smile.

"What am I looking for? I am looking for that tooth that you have lost," I said, and she snapped her mouth shut and covered it with her hand while her sisters laughed.

3

Let the dead Past bury its dead!
Act,—act in the living Present!

—*Longfellow*

THE KATHMANDU OF PRE-COLUMBIAN AMERICA
and the oldest continuously inhabited city in the Western hemisphere lies
in a remote Andean valley 11,000 feet above sea level. Known by the Incas
as Tawantinsuyo, the "Four Quarters of the Earth," the Inca empire once
stretched from Ecuador to Argentina and from the Pacific Ocean to the
Amazon jungle. Cuzco, the "Earth's navel," the Holy City and capital of the
empire, was founded by Manco Capac, the first Inca, the "Son of the Sun,"
sometime around A.D. 1100. Some four hundred years later, Atahuallpa
Inca, the ruler of the empire and descendent of the Son of the Sun, was as-
sassinated there by the handful of Spanish soldiers of fortune led by Captain
Francisco Pizarro, the man who "conquered" Peru.

Pizarro installed an Indian nobleman named Manco as a puppet Inca,
and proceeded to plunder the riches and desecrate the temples of the wondrous alien empire that he had discovered.

But Manco Inca fled Cuzco and raised an army of 100,000 to lay
siege to the city, now teeming with Spanish troops and settlers. Cuzco had
been built in the shape of a jaguar whose back was formed by the Tullumayo
river and whose head was Sacsayhuaman, a hill overlooking the city. It was
there that the fate of the greatest civilization in the Western Hemisphere was
decided in the spring of 1536.

The megalithic temples and towers of Sacsayhuaman, the honeycomb of interconnected chambers behind three tiers of zig-zagging ramparts, became the citadel of the empire when Manco's troops took the hill. From the head of the jaguar, the Indians laid siege to their occupied capital. Though the siege of Cuzco would last for months, it is said that Cuzco burned in a day. In May Francisco Pizarro's brother Juan led his cavalry out from the smoldering seat of the empire to attack Sacsayhuaman.

The battle for Sacsayhuaman, for the head of the jaguar, must certainly have been one of the most desperate and dramatic in history. Like the fires that had consumed Cuzco, Manco Inca's rebellion had spread throughout the country; and for seven days and nights the fate of the empire and the success of the conquest hung in the balance.

Many thousands died in the slaughter at Sacsayhuaman. Once the Spaniards took the outer ramparts, forcing the Indians back into the temples, the heavily armored *conquistadores* began their hand-to-hand execution of the natives. The next morning, while Manco Inca fled for the safety of a fabled jungle redoubt called Vilcabamba, condors feasted on the battleground and soared circling above the head of the fallen jaguar.

Though Manco and his successors waged a vicious guerrilla war against the Spanish colonists and their property for the next forty years, the Inca empire fell at Sacsayhuaman. The three great towers were toppled, the temples were laid waste, and one of the greatest architectural achievements of the ancient world became a rock quarry for the building of Spanish Cuzco.

Today the three-tiered, four-hundred-meter-long, zig-zagging northern ramparts and the outline of the tower bases are all that remain of the head of the jaguar of Cuzco.

You can look down on all of Cuzco from up there, eight hundred feet above the Plaza de Armas at the heart of the city. I used to jog up to the ruins in the mornings years ago, run along the top of the zig-zag ramparts that I fancied as representing the teeth of the jaguar.

At the sunken circular stone foundation of Muyumarca, I would practice *t'ai chi*, the Chinese martial art of movement, for half an hour, moving slowly, sinuously, with the energy of the new day. Sometimes children would watch me, their placid faces cocked to one side, contemplating my strange dance and my preoccupation. Sometimes one would join me, laughing self-consciously at first, mimicking my moves but not mocking me, then continue on down the hill to school or after some errand. And I would walk northeast a few miles to Tambo Machay, the Temple of the Waters, to bathe in the chill spring water before returning to town.

Now, on the evening of my arrival in Cuzco, I sat on a granite slab at the highest point of the ruined citadel and looked down at the city, the lights that issued from or illuminated the facades of countless churches, chapels, ancient palaces, converted temples, historic homes, seminaries, monasteries, markets, hotels, and restaurants. At the center of all this, the Plaza de Armas: the Cathedral, the chapels of Jesus Maria, El Triunfo, and La Compañia, all fashioned from the stones of the great gold-covered Inca palaces and temples they replaced.

There was no trace of Antonio in the city at the foot of the hill. I had traveled here with no conscious agenda, with nothing but a vague sense of purpose. Here I was looking down at the city I knew so well, the place that I will always associate with the greatest adventure of my life. Had I hurried to this place only to gaze upon all those things past?

A shooting star caught my eye. I watched it arc through the sky and flame out in the east near the snowcapped peak of Pachatusan. There was a half moon that night; it was cloudless and the stars sparkled in the near perfect blackness, and what moonlight there was shone silver-white in the thin clean air and defined the stone remnants of Sacsayhuaman in high contrast. Someone was standing there.

A man stood on the rim of the sunken foundation of the circular tower. He stood directly across from me. I could say that he stared at me across the thirty feet that separated us, across the rubble and sparse highland grass and wildflowers, but that would be inaccurate. Though his face was square with mine and his attitude was fixed, strictly speaking he could not stare, although he was not blind.

He wore dry, black, cracked leather shoes but no socks, a pair of old polyester pants, a heavy cotton T-shirt, and a shapeless, threadbare sports jacket that was too small—his thin wrists protruded inches below the cuffs. There was a narrow-brimmed hat with a plaid band on his head. His hands were limp by his sides and hung more than halfway to his knees.

His face was expressionless in the moonlight; for the center of expression is the eyes, and they were nothing but shadows, a blank, shaded place below the brim of the silly hat. He was or had been an Indian, and the gray-white stubble of many days' growth stood out against the dark skin stretched over the hollows below his cheeks.

Another star arced silently across the heavens behind his head, drawing my attention for an instant from his face, and I realized that I had been staring at the place below the brim of the hat. Suddenly, I did not know how long we had stood like this, how long the moment had lasted. And I remembered then that I had seen him before.

I had seen him here on this very spot ten or twelve years ago. Antonio had seen him too. We had been walking back from Tambo Machay. Night had fallen by the time we reached the ramparts and scrambled up the hill to Sacsayhuaman. We had stood as I stood now, watching the lights of the city below. When we had turned to go, he had been there, standing near the base of the fallen tower.

Antonio had touched my arm. "Do not look into its eyes," he said.

And Antonio, professor of philosophy and learned man that he was, had explained to me that this was a "dis-spirited one," a *pischaco*, one who preys on the energy, the life force of others like a vulture, though they are nothing but carrion themselves. The living dead.

I had laughed at him as he whispered this to me that night, when he told me that there are sorcerers who capture their very essence and send these flesh-and-bone golems to wander through the night. "It is popularly believed that these sorcerers extract the body fat from their bodies."

"Zombies?" I had whispered back, grinning back into his earnest eyes. "You're talking about *zombies?*"

"The idea is the same," he nodded. "They cannot walk in a straight line."

"What?" I glanced quickly at the inert figure. Antonio gripped my arm.

"Do not look at it, my friend. Do not look for its eyes or it will capture you with its sightless gaze, and you could lose your soul to it. Only observe. Be still and observe." He had bent over slowly and picked up a stone the size of a fist. "Go!" he said suddenly, and he threw the stone. It struck the man in the chest. There was a hollow thud and the stone fell to the ground at the man's shoes.

"Leave!" Antonio had shouted. It sounded so strange in the night air.

Then the man moved, sideways like a crab, with short jerky movements; with small, awkward steps it stumbled away down the side of the hill.

"Life in death," my friend had said. "Or death in life, I am not sure which is a more appropriate description . . ."

I had passed off the incident long ago, passed it off as a rare and eccentric moment of fancy; I have never thought of Antonio as fallible.

But this thing again stood before me now: animal, vegetable, or mineral, it was he—or *it,* if I can believe in such things. Though some of the clothes had changed, I would swear that he wore the same ruined shoes.

I felt a chill and realized that my pores had opened. There was a cold prickly sweat on my legs, my back, my face.

I turned suddenly and hurried away from there, headed down the hill toward the city rather than along the trail through the ruins, for it was too late and I was done with this place.

Halfway down the hill I turned and looked up. He was gone. And all of a sudden I felt as though there was nothing alive—no living thing within miles—and I ran the rest of the way down the hill.

4

*We assemble our present with the bits and pieces of our past,
seeking to avoid those circumstances that caused us pain,
seeking to recreate those that caused us joy. We are helpless captives.*

—*Antonio Morales*

IT ALL MADE SENSE THE NEXT MORNING; OR AT
least I wrestled it all into something sensible. I awoke in the corner room
of the Hotel los Marqueses, pulled on my trousers, and stumbled sleepily
out onto the balcony for that sweet moment of waking in a new place, beginning a new morning far from the last.

I stood on the balcony over narrow, cobbled Garcilaso Street, and
discovered that the past night's encounter had acquired a significance while
I slept.

According to folklore, that unwholesome and eerie presence in the
ruins could have held me hostage in its gaze and milked me of my spirit. The
message was obvious: Whether I stared into his hollow eyes or into the shadows between the lights of the city that lay in the darkness at my feet, I
stood to lose something of myself.

The notion that the wandering, undead thing was a manifestation of
my unconscious in no way discounts the experience; the thing in the ruins
was real, not spectral—had I thrown a stone, I would have hit something
solid. By the time I finished my first cup of coffee at the Café Roma, I had
invested the incident with significance.

I had journeyed back to Peru with some vague sense of purpose, looking to complete something that I had started so long ago. I was standing on the edge of a cliff, looking back over my shoulder at the trail by which I had come, certain that the trail itself would show me how to take the next step.

So perhaps Antonio's admonition—his melodramatic warning to avert my eyes from the shadow brim of that unnatural thing in the ruins—had been a premonition of this time when I would return alone, seeking something more, fired by expectations based on past adventures, seduced by memories of a past that he and I had shared.

Had I been less susceptible to my own fancies, I might have seen that encounter in the ruins for what it was.

It was life-in-death and death-in-life that had announced itself to me that night at Sacsayhuaman. I know it now; I missed it at the time, just as I might miss the theme of a Stravinsky symphony because I am so preoccupied with the absence of familiar chords.

No matter. My interpretation, fanciful as it was, caused me to make a decision. I finished my breakfast and second cup of coffee and left the Café Roma. I stepped out into the dizzy bright sunlight of the Plaza de Armas and headed for a place that I knew sold maps.

When the Spanish came to Peru, they encountered a people and civilization that defied the European imagination. Here was an empire whose father was the Sun, whose cities of stone and gold were built of and into the Earth.

And here were a people whose features were so noble as to satirize the Romans; their skin glowed not with the pallor of the Moon, but the radiance of the Sun. They covered themselves with fabrics made of silklike wool woven and dyed with the most brazen colors of Nature in patterns of intricate geometry. They adorned themselves with the skins of monstrous reptiles and the feathers and plumes of loud, freakish birds of absurd beauty. They wore hammered gold over their hearts and from their ears. They inhabited a land the size of Spain, Portugal, France, England, and the Austro-Hungarian Empire put together; they ruled from cities in the clouds, from peaks that dwarfed the ranges of Europe; their capital was in a valley higher than any mountain in Spain. They had domesticated over a hundred food products; invented a system of social security; built paved highways, suspension bridges, and tunnels to join their empire. They understood the cycles and moods of the planets. They kept no records. There were only the *quipucamayocs,* the keepers of the oral history and craftsmen of the *quipus,* the color-coded knotted strings that documented events of the past, present, and future. So when the Spanish laid waste to the empire of the Children of the Sun, they obliterated an entire culture. Luckily a handful of Spanish chroniclers managed to record much of what they saw and some of what they heard, though they understood little; for the chronicles document the Conquest rather than the culture it savaged.

The Royal Road of the Incas, the network of paved trail and highway that joined the empire, spanned the 3,250-mile highland route from Ecuador to Chile, and 2,250 miles of the Peruvian coast. Spanish chronicler Pedro de Cieza de León, writing sometime in the 1540s, was perhaps the first European to describe this wonder of the world.

"In the memory of people," wrote Cieza,

> I doubt there is record of another highway comparable to this, running through deep valleys and over high mountains, through piles of snow, quagmires, living rock, along turbulent rivers; in some places it ran smooth and paved, carefully laid out; in others over sierras, cut through the rock, with walls skirting the rivers, and steps and rests through the snow; everywhere it was clean-swept and kept free of rubbish, with lodgings, storehouses, temples to the sun, and posts along the way. Oh, can anything comparable be said of Alexander, or of any of the mighty kings who ruled the world, that they built such a road, or provided the supplies to be found on this one! The road built by the Romans that runs through Spain and the others we read of were as nothing in comparison to this.

These Inca trails were the nervous system of the empire. The Spanish were a seafaring people and were quick to command the coastal highways, and Pizarro would establish his capital at Lima. In the Andes, where the trails often traversed mountainsides thousands of feet above gorges that might have been bottomless for the mists that obscured them, the Royal Road of the Incas was impractical for Spanish horses and caravans. One such trail followed the Urubamba river to Ollantaytambo—the site of savage battles between Pizarro's troops and Manco Inca's guerrilla forces—and then turned north out from the valley and into the jungle. The invading forces apparently never followed the trail that continued on, the left fork in the trail that led past Ollantaytambo, down the valley of the Urubamba, across the river at the Bridge of Joy, and through the Valley of the Rainbows.

This trail, which remained hidden from the Spanish, turned northwest at a place known as Grassy Plain, passed through the Plain of the Llullucha Flower, and climbed to nearly 14,000 feet at Dead Woman's Pass before descending through the Valley of the Rainbows and on for two more days of tangled jungle and high sierras, past temples and shrines and observatory outposts, to a place called the Gateway of the Sun.

This was the way that was kept secret from the Spanish for hundreds of years, an entire region abandoned by the Incas and forgotten by history. It led to a place where the Urubamba curls moatlike around the base of a great pinnacle rising from the valley, a place where the Sun seems always to shine through the clouds that hide the surrounding mountains. There, perched nestlike on the saddle between the twin peaks of the great pinnacle, was a city of astonishing beauty, an aerie of spiritual nobility, where a thousand people worshiped the Sun and the Moon and the Earth.

The trail that led on from Ollantaytambo and over the Bridge of Joy and past the Valley of the Rainbows was the Royal Road to Machu Picchu.

Scarcely half an hour after my breakfast at the Café Roma, I sat on a wrought iron bench in the Plaza de Armas. The map I held unfolded in front of me was of the topographical sort published by government geologic agencies—fine green wavy lines radiating out from tiny triangles that mark the peaks of great mountains. I followed the dotted line that marked the Inca Trail from a place called Corihuayrachina to Machu Picchu. There, at an elevation of 13,860 feet, near the center of the map where a cross oriented you to the cardinal points of the compass, was Huarmihuañusca, Dead Woman's Pass, the place in the snow, the pass in my dreams.

Spent the day hunting up provisions: dried fruit, nuts, peanut butter, dried sausage and cheese, eight cans of soup. Coffee. Toilet paper. The Café Garcilaso across the street has made up a package of *quinoa* flour pancakes—like crepes made from the grain of Andean pigweed. I bought four boxes of coca tea.

Bought another sweater and a pair of alpaca gloves from Angelina the *lanera*. Found an old Primus camp stove, battered brass, the relic of some expedition of the 1930s, the Timex of camp stoves; it still works, though it looks as if it had been dropped from some great height. Bought a hat, a medium-brimmed felt hat with a satin band.

In four days there will be a full moon, and it is said that the best weather for such an expedition is during the last few days before a full moon.

With two canteens, a pot to boil water in, and a pack filled with food and one change of clothes, I have a workout ahead of me. I brought my tent and sleeping bag. I brought my hiking boots from California. I suppose I knew I'd be doing this all along.

Returning to a place that I have been, by a road that I have never traveled. Alone. I will be my own companion: the one that I never see.

PART II

THE OTHER

5

If you do follow your bliss you put yourself on a kind of track that has been there all the while, waiting for you, and the life that you ought to be living is the one you are living ... You begin to meet people who are in the field of your bliss, and ... doors will open where you didn't know they were going to be.

—*Joseph Campbell*

AND SO I SET OUT ON ANOTHER JOURNEY. I TURNED my back on everything that I thought I was looking for and took a walk. I would not be alone for long.

April 20
Day One

The day began in darkness—6:15 A.M. The third-class train from Cuzco to Ollantaytambo stopped for what might have been two minutes at a rustic station on the right bank of the Urubamba. There was just time to get from my seat to the doorway, throw my pack out onto the dirt, and jump off.

I had company there in the dark—*campesinos*—farmers, and two *huayruros,* father and son.

A man and a boy dressed in Quechua-style red woven shirts and snug hood-shaped alpaca caps with ear flaps beaded with red and black; they are *huayruros,* Andean porters who make their living carrying other people's baggage through the mountains. They wore short pants that exposed overdeveloped calves, and sandals that seemed to be fused to the cracked leather soles of their feet; their toenails were thick and ragged and curved like talons. The father offered to take my pack. I answered no with all the Quechua I could manage. He grinned; his teeth were stained with *llibta,* the chunk of lime-rich clay they wrap with coca leaves and chew to stimulate them, to regulate their heart muscle at altitude. They crossed the rusted suspension bridge over the Urubamba with me, then disappeared in the deep gray predawn shadows of a valley.

I headed southeast, following an easy trail across a tiny stream and above a grove of eucalyptus.

Dawn broke late in the Valley of the Urubamba. As I made my way upstream, I watched as the Sun rose behind and to the left of Veronica, the great 18,000-foot snow-covered *apu,* "caretaker" of the Sacred Valley. I saw the great cumulus clouds that scudded across the peak glow pink and orange, backlit by the Sun, while long rays of light defined by morning mist moved dutifully down the right-hand side of the valley. When the Sun finally broke over the horizon so far above me, the jagged snowcap of Veronica glowed golden.

At dawn I reached the ruins of Llactapata, a citadel embedded in the hillside at the mouth of the valley where the Cusichaca flows into the Urubamba. I did not stop, but descended to the river and crossed it at a place marked by an Inca buttress, followed a simple path traversing the left side of the valley.

It has been an easy day. The Cusichaca Valley is high sierra and rugged: cactus and pigweed and thorny *kiswar* and *chilca* shrubs. The valley narrows gradually and the growth thickens with *cachaco-moc* trees, deep green leaves and paperlike bark shedding in long peels. At 8,000 or 9,000 feet above sea level, the air is not a problem; I have descended from Cuzco.

Alone. Perhaps *I* am the Other of my dreams. He whom I pursue and who pursues me. No cat-and-mouse game today. I was simply thankful to be here, grateful to the undead thing at Sacsayhuaman for snapping me out of the hypnotic spell of the last few years. I don't fully understand why I came to Peru this time, and I no longer care, but I know that I did not rush here for the fool's gold at Sipan.

Here, though, my mind is free to be with itself. Only my body is occupied: my legs working rhythmically in cadence with my arms, I move along a pathway that I see stretching ahead of me through the gentle gray-green valley, and my mind is free to turn on itself. Somehow here I cannot think of mundane things. Already, in one day, I have found an intimacy and clarity to the quality of my thoughts.

Today I spent my time reasoning out my profession.

I am a psychologist, a doctor of psychology; I have been trained in and have taught the traditions of that Western discipline. *Doctor* is the only formal title in common usage in the United States; it is particularly coveted by those physicians and academicians of the "hard sciences." Ever since Freud, the assumption of the title by those who study the human psyche has been met with some disdain. One never hears of pop-biology, pop-physiology, or pop-medicine. There is a popular belief that since psychology is the study of the source of subjective thought and abstract interpretation, psychology does not qualify as a science; and if they give out doctorates in psychology, they might as well hand them out to astrologers as well.

Psychology is literally the study of the psyche, variously defined as the human soul, the spirit, and the mind. Psychology is the study of something that modern science has failed to identify. The mind is thought to reside in the brain, but we cannot prove that it does. We can dissect, grind up, weigh the human brain, measure its electromagnetic fields, and monitor its molecular biological behavior, but the mind evades us. The properties of awareness cannot be derived from the neurology of the human brain. We can no more locate the center of consciousness than we can prove the existence of God. We know that we have a mind—our mind tells us that we do—but it does not reveal itself to hypothesis, clinical validation, and independently repeatable results.

Inescapably, when we study the human mind, it is the mind that is studying itself. This is the paradox of the science of psychology: If the human brain were so simple that we could understand it, we would be so simple that we couldn't.

Contemporary Western psychology is practiced clinically, statistically, and behaviorally. Its foundation—its image and metaphor base—was laid down by Freud as the result of his studies of the dreams and psyches of disturbed patients. Psychology's first practitioners, the shamans, practice the discipline from an altogether different angle. The tradition of shamanism is the practice of experiential psychology. Its images and metaphors are drawn from the most creative and artistic minds of the community. The symbols and archetypes of their psychology represented what the shaman saw and experienced while journeying fearlessly through the domains of consciousness.

Furthermore Western psychology is built upon a myth of origin that condemns its people as outcasts from Paradise, from Nature. Consequently Western therapy is obsessed with treating the neuroses of a people who were ousted from Paradise into a hostile world—first by God and later by their parents. And we have embodied the myth. So distant and separate from Nature have we become that not even the incest taboo, Nature's prime directive, functions among our people. In every corner of the world, incest is punishable by death or banishment; yet 30 percent of the American population has been sexually abused by a parent who has gone unpunished. In contrast, the psychology of the Native Americans is founded on a mythology that describes man and woman walking in beauty on a loving mother, the Earth, and under the nourishing paternal gaze of the Sun.

> I ate at mid-afternoon. Had forgotten to eat, so filled was I with reflection. I reached a small tributary and crossed a log bridge and followed the right-hand side of the valley until I came to the tiny settlement of Huayllabamba. Like its name, it is a small grassy plain, a primitive burial ground where a thatched-roof stone hut serves as a one-room schoolhouse for the Indians of the Valley of the Llullucha Flower.

I made camp near the schoolhouse, pitched my tent at the base of a hill where there are the scattered ruins of an old cemetery. I pumped the tiny piston of the old Primus camp stove, filled my pot with water from the stream, liberally dosed it with tincture of iodine, and watched the water boil.

So it is the end of the first day and I have eaten and the Sun has set over the high horizon and the cold is setting in. I will not light a fire here, but write by the poor light of the camp stove. I am boiling coca tea that will cool by morning, and I'll fill my canteens with it—an acquired taste, even its color is yellow-green bilious—but it refreshes; and if it gives me a lift, I don't notice.

A few minutes ago I saw two boys, Indians, leading a swaybacked horse through the cemetery on the hill behind me.

I am very tired. Alone but not lonely. It is cold, and the blackness of the night is as complete as the brilliance of the day at this unpolluted altitude. The stars of night are more distinct than the star of day; they stand out in the utter blackness. They seem closer, surely not because I am 9,000 feet nearer to them, but because the light that reaches me does not pass through the dense recycled air of the lower regions where most of the world lives. The star of the day, the Sun, is less distinct here; its brightness fills the sky with such unfiltered light that it is hard to distinguish its face—it is simply the brightest part of the brightest sky I will ever see.

I wish that I could tell of a dream that I had, another installment in the serial that I had dreamed in San Francisco and in Canyon de Chelly. The fact is that I slept like a log that night.

Overslept. I jerked awake—which is unusual when sleeping out of doors—and let my head fall back on the rolled-up trousers I used for a pillow. The Sun had penetrated the valley, and the atmosphere in my tent was blue because the fabric was a filter for the light. I lay there breathing in the blue, stale air and made a cautious inventory of my body: calves, thighs, shoulders. Too much exercise, like too much wine, makes me apprehensive on the morning after. But I was fine.

If only I had not overslept. Today's leg would be longer, steeper, higher than yesterday's, and I knew that I must reach the pass before sunset.

I had slept on my watch, and when I found it I scrambled to my knees and unzipped myself from the tent. It was quarter after nine.

The boys were back; the two boys with the swaybacked horse stood on the hill behind me, the burial ground, and watched me while their horse chewed on something. The schoolyard was deserted; the schoolhouse that looked like a thatched-over Inca ruin was vacant, and the only sound on the grassy plain was the sound of the water of the Llulluchayoc running under the footbridge.

I should have eaten; but the need to make some way, to put some distance between me and the place I had stopped, had me yanking on my clothes, wrestling the tent into its bag, stuffing my sleeping bag, filling my canteens with the coca tea I had brewed the night before, harnessing on my pack, and on the trail by quarter to ten.

So I left the valley late that morning and managed incidentally to entertain the two little boys who watched my determined hastiness with expressionless curiosity, like the children who watched me dance *t'ai chi* at Sacsayhuaman. Back then it was a North American practicing Chinese movement among the ruins of ancient Peru. Here it was a *gringo* acting as though he were late for something in the middle of the Andes, where late and early qualify the time of day, not the condition of a man. They sat enthralled on the hill among the cactus and *kiswar* shrubs and tumbled-down walls of the cemetery. They were gone by the time I left.

I climbed the hill and skirted the shapeless ruins and began to ascend a grade, unrelenting and densely forested. The trail, a dirt trail—there are few signs of paved Inca road here—rises forever, and I felt the effects of the altitude, the weight of my pack, my hunger, the slow aching burn of lactic acid in my legs, the strain of my lungs against my rib cage. I was working hard now to get to where I was going, and the sweatband of my hat was soaked, the satin stained with salty white outlines, and the foam-packed nylon shoulder straps and kidney pads of my pack were damp sponges by the time I reached the lush green glade where the Llulluchayoc converges with the Huayruro Chico.

An Andean sort of paradise at the mouth of two steep-sided and deep green valleys; there is a patch of long grass where the streams meet. There are canary yellow and cardinal red *k'antu* flowers, the lemon-flavored stems of *ajhu-ajhu,* and everywhere the *llullucha* herb, bell-shaped with clusters of purple berries. The Spanish moss starts here in a tangle of oaklike *mark'u* trees, *chachacomoc,* and the last of the thorny *kiswars.* The earth is soft and pulpy; it still guards the moisture of the March rains.

I dropped my pack, separated my hat from the matted hair at my temples, and peeled off my shirt. I pulled off my boots and thick socks and ducked under a low-slung branch of a patriarchal *mark'u* tree, and waded gingerly into the icy, sparkling stream. I bathed myself using my old bandanna as a washcloth, then soaked it, wrung it out, twirled it, and tied it around my neck.

I doused my shirt and hung it from the branch of the *mark'u* tree, and breakfasted while it dried.

A late breakfast of dried fruit and cold *quinoa* pancakes. No time for coffee because of my late start. I must reach Dead Woman's Pass before sunset.

A few extra moments to fill with writing while my shirt fails to dry.

The novelty of the first day's trek has worn off, and I am staring at a long walk ahead.

An hour ago, passed by the ruins of a small Inca settlement nestled into the valley. There are more ruins ahead, but they are beyond the pass.

I tell myself that I have abandoned all thoughts of a goal, purpose, reason for this solo expedition. I know only that Machu Picchu waits for me at the end; I have my curiosity about the pass I will ascend today, and the thought of another man hiking this trail, dogging my footsteps or waiting for me at a bend in the stream is pure melodrama.

I am indulging myself. The physical demands of walking this way and the unique beauty of the land my trail passes through are enough to preoccupy me. And there *are* the little goals: the next rise, that clump of rock or bend in the trail or strange looking flower *just* ahead. Make it there before stopping . . .

I dressed and hoisted my pack and followed the left fork of the river to a log bridge, where the trail became more distinct. Here I ascended to a bluff, and three remarkable birds—emerald green and crimson, with tiny bright yellow beaks and ridiculously long tail feathers—flew, flapping in formation down the valley.

I followed the trail that winds through thick forest, tropical, tangled, deep green vegetation: Spanish broom and tree ferns, *chacomo* trees with paperlike bark, rotting logs and moldering undergrowth, everywhere bright splashes of yellow and orange lichen. The trail led down, back to the Llulluchayoc, and I followed the left bank of the riverbed for the whole of that afternoon.

If I spent most of that first day, the easy day, getting accustomed to walking, and thinking about the purpose of psychology, I spent the second day testing my endurance and my resolve, and thinking about what I had done to fulfill my purpose.

I have sought experiences and attempted to serve them. Antonio once told me that the difference between an experience and an experience served was determined by the purity of one's intent. An experience will not serve you if you do not serve the experience. The example he used the first time he explained it was the Holy Communion. I admitted that I had taken the sacrament; the wafer was tasteless and strange in my mouth and the wine was cheap and too sweet. He pointed out that had I invested myself in the odd ritual of eating the body and drinking the blood of Christ, I might have had an experience of communion with an enlightened state. There is a purpose to such a ritual that is missed if one's intent is not in harmony with the experience. It was so like Antonio to cite an example from a philosophy that he would one day so elegantly expose.

But an experience does not need to be a ritual, ceremony, or anything conceived as significant in order for it to be served. The trap, of course, is that every encounter we have is, strictly speaking, an *experience*. One must be able to distinguish between those experiences that are worth serving and those that are not. It requires a certain state of awareness—a discretionary instinct; otherwise one ends up investing every moment with profound meaning, and the most wearisome people in the world are those who are utterly unconscious and those who are hyperconscious.

Long ago I had determined my purpose: to find a way to study consciousness, a method that would reveal more than the scientific method that restricts the study of the mind to objective analysis. My intent was to find a way to translate such a method, if it existed, into a modern Western practice. I followed the pathways laid down by the first psychologists, those who explored the human mind from the inside out rather than the outside in. I soon discovered that I required a new state of mind: one that allows for subjective experiences but is not beguiled by them. I found that the skills needed to develop such a state of mind were acquired along the pathway of served experiences; they came naturally. It was like finding a machete waiting for you just where the path becomes tangled and impenetrable. So I proceeded to craft a mind that might support a wholesome and responsible exploration of the human mind and its capabilities, and sought experiences that would serve to test my limits. Some of them were shocking; most of them were out of the ordinary. I experienced my visual reality altered by a painfully dramatic ritual, and found that I could perceive the ebb and flow of subtle biological energies. I learned to walk in an animistic world where I could perceive the enchantment of the rocks and trees and clouds, where the mountains were great *apus,* and the rivers and ravines were powerful *aukis.*

I experienced my own death and wandered through a land of archetypal figures that seemed to exist in a world created by life itself, parallel to the world of the familiar. I left my dead body moldering in the sands of a desert at the bottom of an Amazonian lagoon and "lived" to tell about it.

I learned something of what it is to dream awake, and found that it is possible to interact with the images created by the mind and by Nature. I experienced myself in other forms: animal forms that could travel independent of my body. I witnessed events that suggested that time and space *are* flexible, and understood why physicists are becoming the philosophers and poets of science.

I made love with a woman—at once a maiden and an old crone—who stepped out from the Pachamama Stone in Machu Picchu. And my "hallucination" was witnessed by a friend who stood by me all through that night. He described to me the details of an experience that I had assumed was private, subjective, altogether my own.

Random highlights of fifteen years of rare perceptions and perspectives, of remarkable healings and precognitive displays and all the other bells and whistles of mysticism that are taken for granted as a by-product of the shamanic state of mind.

Predictably I found that I could *serve* an experience by capturing it, preparing it, and presenting it, ungarnished, for consumption. Food for thought. Ultimately I "served" my experiences by telling them, by translating them into a chronicle.

But there is no accounting for taste. Some would find the meal unsavory. Others would *acquire* a taste for it. For some it was hard to digest. And then, of course, there are some people who will eat anything.

Some complained that some of the dishes were over-seasoned. Seasoning, they argued, can bring out the flavor of a dish and it can alter its taste entirely. Mind-altering substances, like herbs and spices, can turn the bland and unexceptional into the tasteful but essentially unauthentic. To those critics it was no matter that the meal as a whole did not depend on its seasonings. My adventures in the realms of shamanic consciousness never *depended* upon the *ayahuasca* and San Pedro, the native "medicines" that I had used. How *little* they depended upon them I had yet to discover.

April 21
Day Two

Followed the left bank of the Llulluchayoc for hours. Hot and heavy work, but I feel as though I have passed through an enchanted forest. It is a perfectly clear day, and the unfiltered Sun fills the sky with a dazzling white brightness that penetrates even the tangle of leaves and branches and vines and half-fallen trunks and hanging moss. Even in the most obscure hollows of the forest, there is a crisp distinctness to every detail: the textures of rotting bark and fungus, flower petals and translucent new growth, mossy granite, glistening stones. The colors intoxicate—every shade of green and brown and yellow and red, so rich and lustrous that they could set the standard for the spectrum.

I have emerged from this wood by climbing a steep trail up through the edge of the trees to a sloping and multileveled zone of pasture. I have stopped to eat at the first of these natural terraces. This is Llulluchapampa, the Plain of the Llullucha Flower.

A commanding view back down the way I have come, back down the valley. In the distance Huayanay, the 19,000-foot *apu,* a glistening white snowbound peak; and beyond and to the left, Veronica. Ahead of me, where I must go, I cannot see the peaks of Llullucha and Huayruro because of the bend in the valley, but I know that they are there. The pass, Huarmihuañusca, goes between them.

Looking back at the way I have come; leading my modern mind along a very old pathway.

When I reach my journey's end, I will be able to describe what I saw: the gentle slope of the pathway that traverses a hillside of mesquite and cactus just above the floor of a valley where the Cusichaca River flows south-southwest; the place where the Cusichaca meets the Llulluchayoc, and the valley named for that flower that ascends through a magical forest and leads to a high Andean pass. These things I have already seen, and there is so much more ahead of me: other valleys to explore, forests to penetrate, cliff sides to scale, ruins to wander through. All of them, all of these wondrous things, to be found in a remote mountain range where the Earth itself reaches up into the clouds.

I will be able to describe it all, to name the jagged snowcapped peaks, characterize the terrain, identify the plants and animals that live here.

Like an early pioneer, I can return to my home and relate my journey to people who have not had the luxury of such a trip, who have not created the opportunity to experience such a thing for themselves. And they will take my word for it. They will know that if they were to take such a trip, they would see what I have seen with my own two eyes. And my experience would help them to find their way. They might even grow confident in their ability to withstand the effects of the altitude, the tropical latitude, the intensity of thinly filtered solar radiation.

No one would question me.

And why should they? I would simply be describing what I saw with my own two eyes.

And we all know that we have two eyes. We only suspect that there is another way of seeing. We don't understand it yet, and so we refuse to acknowledge *those* visions, the lessons they teach, the questions they pose and those they answer.

The Sun was dangerously low in the white sky when I left the plain. Bearing to the left, I continued an unrelenting ascent up the valley. Perhaps an hour passed before I realized that everything had changed.

Llulluchapampa was a transitional zone between the high valley forest and the *puna*, the treeless grasslands of the high Andes. The valley was broad and grassy at the bottom, and the walls rose russet gray and on either side. And now the climb was steep—steeper than the gradual rise of a valley floor where the river ran.

I found myself watching my boots tread the pathway. I became conscious of my breathing and the pounding of my heart and the need to stop. Instead I raised my head, looked up. Then I stopped—not because of the fatigue, but because of what I saw: the trail that continued to rise mercilessly before me, a pathway scratched into the face of a barren mountainside, a granite-studded escarpment of terra-cotta-colored soil, and the stubble of highland grass rising a thousand feet to the snow line. I could not see the peak of Huayruro, though I walked along its northeastern slope.

I blinked the sweat from my eyes, pulled off my hat, and wiped my face with my forearm. To the right, across the valley, another ridiculously steep slope rising to scattered ice patches to the snowbound peak of Llullucha. Directly ahead, maybe half a mile away, the saddle-shaped pass level with the snow line. This was Huarmihuañusca, Dead Woman's Pass.

From where I stood, squinting up at the trail, the angle of ascent was exaggerated. I estimated my elevation at something less than 13,000 feet; the pass was 13,860. If I had 1,000 vertical feet to climb and I was 2,500 feet away, the angle would be between 20 and 25 degrees. That wasn't so bad.

But at altitude, all my calculations were just numbers. Already the shadows were moving along the slopes of the valley. I had to get there. I could do it in time if I did it steadily, resolutely, if I concentrated on moving—to that place just below the pass where the trail turned sharply left, heading for the center of the saddle. There was a flat place there; it would be my goal; I would need a second, even third wind to make it; but once there I knew I could push myself, surely, to the summit.

I took one last look around. The valley was perfectly still; no breeze to move the thin, precious air. Back along the trail the tree line seemed much farther below me than I had imagined, and this cheered me. There was no sign of the man who followed me in my dream, the superhuman trekker who passed me and pitched my tent in the Pacamayo Valley beyond the pass while I slept there. Had I really expected to hear the scrape of his boots on the scant paving stones of this trail? I looked for the condor. There had been a condor in my dream, soaring in low circles over the pastureland that ran up the valley basin. Nothing moved but my heart, thudding 140 or 150 beats per minute, working harder even at rest to carry oxygen through my body.

A body at rest tends to remain at rest.

The sweatband of my hat was cold on my forehead. I pulled the brim down and hooked my thumbs under the straps of my pack and shrugged all fifty pounds of it up onto my shoulders and took the first step.

And the next. Two. Three.

First there was the pass ahead and slope that rose like a wall to my left and fell away to the valley floor at my right; the opposite slope and the twenty feet of rough brick-dust-red path ahead of me. Of these things I had a peripheral awareness. Then . . .

There was only the path strewn with jagged stones and baked-earth dirt. My focus narrowed such that I could only see a couple of yards ahead of me, watch the stones and pebbles that my boots scuffed skittering along before me. Then . . .

There were only my boots moving with time, one breath per step. The rhythm entranced me until I watched them move from a distance and then . . .

There was only I. My body agonizing, the vehicle that carries the awareness of itself straining, all those moving parts aching with effort and my heart hammering, my lungs pumping to keep the body moving.

Antonio once said that there was a way of seeing the totality of a thing. Ordinary seeing was two-dimensional, a picture of a scene. Vision, on the other hand, allowed you to see not only the face of the mountain, for instance, but its every aspect, front and back and sides, from above and below. The eyes, he explained, were not enough; vision was seeing with all of the senses.

This was not the time to experiment. Try as I did to expand my vision, the pounding of my heart was a drum that called me back to my body and the moment. Rather than expand, my awareness contracted: first there was the goal, then there was the path, then there was I. All paths lead to the self.

I actually thought this at the time. Moments of crisis seem always to prompt banalities: You'll get through this; things could be worse; it'll all look different in the morning; it's always darkest before the light; all paths lead to the self . . . My heart and lungs were working three times harder than normal, because at 13,000 feet there is only one-half the oxygen the body needs—and I was moving, not resting, and I had used up all the winds that I had counted on.

And then I stopped. My head swam; the path fell away from me; I had a glimpse of the snow line, and I fell. Luckily I fell to my left, against the slope, which was almost vertical there.

I doubled over: hands on knees, elbows locked . . . until everything stopped moving, and I checked for symptoms of altitude sickness. But there was no nausea, no headache, only the passing dizziness and the raw pain in my lungs and the pummeling of my heart. I knew that if I took off my pack I'd never get it on again.

And then I looked up. Reluctantly I turned my head to look up the path, and I was thirty feet from the bend in the trail, fifty yards from the snow line and the summit. I checked my watch and realized that I had walked for five minutes short of an hour.

The rest of the way was easy.

Huarmihuañusca, Dead Woman's Pass, was the same gentle, saddle-shaped place that I had dreamed of: the soil near the snow line more gray than red, the narrow-blade, needlelike highland grass growing in tufts everywhere; and the pass was sort of gray-green, bounded on either side by the white snow and wind-polished ice.

6

*If you know the adversary and know yourself, you need not fear
the outcome of one hundred battles. If you know yourself but not the
adversary, for every victory gained you will also suffer a defeat.
If you know neither the adversary nor yourself,
you will succumb in every battle.*

—*Sun Tzu*

I DID NOT THROW OFF MY PACK AND DROP TO MY
knees. This was not a dream. I unscrewed the cap of my canteen and took
a long breathless drink of cold coca tea. I just stood there; I must have
stood for a quarter of an hour at the crest of Huarmihuañusca, entranced by
the height as much as by the romantic vista before me.

Huarmihuañusca

Over two and a half miles above sea level, where airplane cabins are
pressurized, where clouds live.

Feeling pretty pleased with myself. In fact, if my dreams brought me
here to push myself to limits, to see what I am seeing, feel what I am
feeling—if only these things and nothing more—then I am satisfied
and even grateful.

I am essentially content here. Behind me is the long Valley of the
Llullucha Flower and the *apus* of Veronica and Huayanay—the
"caretakers" of the way I have come. Before me is the Valley of the

Rainbows, the Pacamayo Valley. And ahead there are the *apus* of Salcantay to the west and the twin peaks of Pyramika and Pumacillo to the northeast—the caretakers of the way I will go. Their white peaks, the underbellies of the clouds, the air itself, it seems, are tinted sunset red, orange, and rose.

The Pacamayo Valley is a romantic place, deep green and forested and tropical, as it follows the Pacamayo River down from a high mountain lake hidden in a fold of the mountain to my left. I have pinpointed it on my map.

Directly across from me I can see the second pass, tomorrow's nemesis: Runkuracay. And below, halfway up the steep slope opposite me are the ruins of Runkuracay. From here they look like a circular pile of stones arranged meticulously on a hillside, like a trail marker along a pathway.

I will camp at a spot almost directly below the ruins. There is a sort of natural terrace by the river and just above the tree line of the tropical-looking forest that overwhelms the descending end of the Valley of the Rainbows.

The Sun is disappearing behind the distant pass. I can't stay here, but must head down the steep slope before me, down the steps of interlocking granite that begin here.

I practically ran down the slope and into the Valley of the Rainbows. Here and there, short flights of Inca-paved steps—interlocking, close-fitted, weatherworn blocks of granite four to six feet wide—slowed my reckless descent, but I was hurrying to reach the campsite I had spotted from the pass. I skipped over an icy stream and ignored the faint path that followed it down the valley into a confusion of vines and tangled undergrowth, and followed the main path above the tree line. In spite of my exhaustion I was exhilarated, eager to reach that place of rest across the river—

It was the waterfall that stopped me. I lurched to a stop, breathless, and the momentum of my backpack almost toppled me. I caught my balance and my breath and stood, steadying myself on the rocky incline, grinning up at the cataract half a mile up the valley and to my left: a fall of water, a narrow stream cascading, free-falling a hundred or two hundred feet down the vertical mountainside. The valley was already in sunset-tinted shadow; there was a rosy hue to all the greens that filled the valley and covered its hillsides and the sight of the falls filled me with such a sense of romance and exotic adventure that I laughed aloud.

I crossed the Pacamayo River at a swampy place of mud and reeds on the valley floor and followed its left bank to the little terrace that I had pinpointed from the pass. I dropped my pack there. Ahead of me, down the sloping valley floor, was dense forest that became jungle. I thought I heard a monkey—something screamed—from down there where it was already dark. This tropical forest filled the valley below for as far as I could see. Eventually, of course, it left the valley and grew even denser, joining the greater jungle, which was warmer, wetter, darker than its higher-altitude fingers, which groped up into countless valleys like this one. There was something menacing about it.

I fired up the old Primus and fetched water from the ice-cold river that burbled and splashed along the rocks, set it to boil, and made a three-foot-diameter circle of stones to contain a fire.

I was ravenous, but it was growing dark and it would be cold soon—colder than the schoolyard at Huayllabamba; the proximity of the tropical forest made me uneasy and reminded me that I was alone here. I needed a fire, its light, warmth, and companionship. So, despite my strange mistrust of the dark tangled branches and dense undergrowth of the tree line that began so suddenly just below my little terrace, I penetrated its edge in search of wood and dry grass.

I made three trips. The moon, nearly full now, rose over Llullucha. The sounds of my footsteps, the breaking branches, cracking and snapping wood, and rustling leaves yanked reluctantly from the tangle all sounded uncomfortably loud, amplified by the stillness of the approaching night—sounds captured by and echoed in the valley.

On my third trip I grasped a dry and hefty looking length of wood and pulled at it—only it was a liana, a thick vine endless in its lithe insinuation of the forest—and when I pulled, it was like pulling a varicose vein from its flesh; the whole tree line resisted—reacted to me. I could not get out of there fast enough. As I scrambled up the little embankment and over a broken-down wall of granite stones—too ill-made to be ancient—I felt something at my back: that sense that runs up the spine . . . that sensitive place that runs from the neck to the tailbone tingled. Maybe it was the forest scolding me.

Soon enough there was a fire filling the circle of stones. I sat close to it and ate slices of sausage and hunks of cheese. There were sounds from the forest—no telling how far away, for I suspected that the shape of the valley distorted sound: birds shrieking and singing, bugs whirring and clicking in the night, that peculiar rhythm and harmony that seems to go so well with the stars and the darkness and the crackling of the fire.

But there was something else, something not appropriate to the conditions, something infecting the air with a presence that did not belong there. And I was dreading it. Dreading something but not knowing what form it would take. And when the voice came out of the night, I came out of my skin; my reaction was involuntary, fight or flight, life or death.

It was the sound of a human voice where there could not have been one, the sight of a human face discovered by the light of the fire—a disembodied dark orange mask, motionless over my right shoulder.

I have heard of sudden terror turning people's hair white at the roots. There is a drastic biochemical reaction to acute fear, and I have no doubt that it is somehow exacerbated by the circumstances—the condition of the body when the fright occurs. Anxiety and anticipation flay the senses. In the night, when danger is looming, you can see in the dark; your dilated pupils probe the blackness for any change in its density; you can hear the softest footfall or the sound of something breathing; you can smell your own sweat; you can feel the air on the back of your neck; you can taste the anxiety itself. And when it happens, when what you dread most reaches out and touches you in the darkness . . .

So involuntary was my reaction that for a moment it was as if I were separate from the 175 pounds of me that shivered as it jerked around to face the fire-lighted face that hovered just behind me.

I gripped my hunting knife—caked with cheese and gleaming with sausage grease—in my right hand; the other hand went to the ground to lever me up but landed on one of the stones that ring the fire.

I screamed a curse of pain and adrenaline rage.

He could have said anything over my shoulder; as I have said, there was something in the air that night and I was poised on the edge of my senses. He could have said anything.

"*Buenas noches—*"

—is what he said, and I spun around and burnt my hand on the rock and pointed my cheese-smeared greasy knife at him and shouted something less than human.

It was a young Indian face, dark orange in the light of the fire. I let out the air trapped in my lungs, got to my feet, and got a grip on myself and my injured hand. "*Perdóne, señor,*" he said, and again a vertical chill passed through me at the sound of his voice. There was nothing wrong with his voice; it was pleasant, in fact. I heard enough of it over the course of the next two days that I can recall its medium pitch and low tone. "Pardon me," he said, and he seemed genuinely concerned at my reaction: his eyes widened and he took a step back. Then his eyes dropped to the fire behind me. He said: "You have dropped something."

I looked behind me. The length of sausage that my left hand had held was blistering in the fire; the skin was swelling and a blister rose and popped with a sizzle of splattered grease.

"Damn!"

I stabbed it with my knife and held it up between us and we both stared at it for a moment before laughing at the absurd looking victim of our encounter.

I should have studied him more carefully, memorized his features and his characteristics, but I had no premonition of him, no inkling of the need I would have in the future to remember him vividly. I failed to register his importance; I failed to *know* that one day I would need to understand him. I am usually good at such things—have been for years; it is a by-product of my training that I can sense the importance of people and events as they cross my path. But I failed that night perhaps because my senses, all six or seven or eight of them, had been stretched taut and had snapped back and left me numb, unaware even of my lack of awareness.

Even now his countenance lacks focus in my memory's eye. He was young, maybe nineteen or twenty. He had refined, almost noble Quechua Indian features. I remember most clearly his hair, long and black and straight (he had the habit of combing it back from his forehead with his hand), and his eyes, clear, dark, and rounder than most Indian eyes.

We ate together. He was half a day ahead of me; he had reached Dead Woman's Pass about the time I had stopped at Llulluchapampa. Instead of skipping over the first stream on his descent into the valley, instead of keeping to the left above the tree line, he had followed that first trail that parallels the stream and leads down into dense jungle. The stream, he told me, eventually disappears underground deep within the forest. It had taken hours for him to disentangle himself and make his way back up the valley. There were traces of ruins in the jungle, he said, but the way was so perilous, full of snakes, the growth was so thick that at times you could not tell whether you were treading on ground or on a natural mat of interwoven vines and branches and leaves two or three feet above the soil. He had no flashlight, but soon after the darkness had closed in around him he had seen my fire.

For all of his adventures in the jungle, he did not seem much the worse for wear. His clothes were old but clean; he wore a heavy charcoal gray alpaca poncho over an alpaca sweater and a pair of jeans. He wore old-fashioned hiking boots—the sort that I associate more with construction work than trekking; and he carried a rucksack—an old army surplus canvas pack—on his back. Hardly the character in my dreams (although I never saw *his* face), but the irony of meeting him here in the Valley of the Rainbows was not lost on me. Later, when I told him about those dreams, those premonitions of an encounter with another along the Inca Trail, he drew his head back and cocked it ever so slightly—a timeless gesture of clinical assessment and mild suspicion. But that was the next day or the day after, I cannot remember which.

That night we spoke of this and that, made a stab at getting to know each other. Despite the fact that I am a psychologist and skilled at gleaning information from others, I realize now that he learned more about me than I about him. He was a student, nearly twenty years my junior, well-educated and very well spoken; and perhaps it was just that education that predisposed him to be suspicious of the *gringo*. Even though I am Latin American by birth, my ancestors are Spanish—*conquistadores, mixti*. And I am from the United States; the world that I represent is certainly first world, jaded, elitist . . . mercenary. My new friend was Quechua by birth, liberal by orientation. I decided early on that he distrusted me, and I suppose that I respected him for it.

"Why do you do this?" he asked, while fiddling with one of the collapsible flexible struts of my tent. We had eaten together—learned the basics about each other. I was Cuban by birth; I was a psychologist from California who had spent many years in Peru. He was a student planning on leaving his country for a "higher education." Tomorrow's coca tea was brewing in the pot on the Primus; the fire was stoked, and we were busy rigging the tent.

"I've always wanted to," I shrugged. "I've been to Machu Picchu many times, but never—"

"Pardon me," he said, "I am asking about your work, not your pleasure."

This stopped me. I was frankly jarred by his rudeness; Latins are forever polite, and direct questions are thought to be impertinent. And this from a stranger, a young man half my age. I glanced over at him and his eyes were wide with something like genuine curiosity.

"Why am I a psychologist?"

He nodded and grinned politely. I smiled back at him.

Pacamayo River Valley

Why am I a psychologist?

Because it was the easiest subject to major in when I realized that I would not follow in my father's footsteps?

Because it is such a flexible discipline: subjective, based on unproved theory, vague, malleable, so susceptible to interpretation?

Because it is the discipline with the fewest rules?

Because the therapist engages with people, many people, on a level of intimacy too rarely experienced in relationship?

None of the above. It is simply what I do best. It thrills me.

The Other of my dreams has turned out to be an eighteen- or twenty-year-old Indian, an earnest young student who will probably leave his country and go to mine to make a future for himself. When I was a student, I left my country for his.

He is sleeping now, wrapped in his poncho by the fire. I offered to share my tent, because he is less equipped for hiking and camping and it is cold. He was too proud to accept. Good for him.

He asked me why I was a psychologist.

"Because," I said, "it makes me think about what I feel, and feel something for what I think." Very glib: a rude answer to an impolite question.

He frowned and nodded as though he were really considering my response. Perhaps he was. Perhaps I had misjudged his earnestness.

"It is like studying the history of my people, though, is it not?" He threw another branch on the fire and watched intently as its leaves browned and curled and its ends caught flame, glowed, turned to ash.

"Your people?"

"The Incas." He cocked his head back in the direction of Runkuracay, now a dark huddled mass on the moonlit hillside behind him. He stared into the fire and his melancholy broke. He grinned widely and looked directly at me. "It has been said that the history of the Incas is 60 percent speculation, 30 percent probability, and 10 percent fact."

"There you have it," I said.

"But why study them? We know that the time of the Incas is past, and we cannot experience their time; but we waste *our* time studying the ruins of *their* time and treating broken-down walls and stones as if they were clues to how they lived."

I took the tent strut and slid it into its sleeve. "I am not studying the history of the Incas," I said.

"I am," he said. He took a long breath and let it out as he said: "And I do not know why."

So I met someone walking this trail after all. So what? I have shown him the hospitality of my fire. We have eaten together.

I hope he is gone in the morning.

I tucked away my journal and twisted the end of my flashlight to shut it off, and the silver moonlight shone faintly bluish gray through one side of my tent; the light of the fire was dull orange on the other side. I hoped that he would be gone in the morning because I was not particularly anxious to share the rest of my journey with anyone. Funny that I had been so pre-occupied with my aloneness only two days before, and now I was relishing it. Besides, he was of a new generation: confused, angry, arrogant, more mature than I had been at his age, because world news and information traveling near the speed of light had bombarded even Peru. This is not to say that I instantly pigeonholed my young friend as an anesthetized cynic, a world-weary, aimless adolescent; on the contrary, his curiosity and initiative to walk among the ruins of his ancestors was admirable; the fact that he did not know why he was here, that he seemed judgmental of his own interest, was disturbing. I was, I suppose, dismayed by an encounter with one who respected his history, but suspected his own values.

Maybe, I thought, as I drew my sleeping bag closer, I'm getting old, failing to understand such confusion and self-scrutiny, such discomfort. No, that wasn't it; I am surely as reckless and doubting as I ever was. Maybe it was merely that he had raised the question of purpose for me again and I was the one who was uncomfortable with my present lack of agenda, in spite of how content I was to be here.

I woke up to my memory of the night before. And I hoped that he was gone all over again. I lay motionless in my tent. It was early, only 6:30, and the predawn chill was, I knew, waiting for me to slip out of my sleeping bag and into all the clothes that I would shed as the sun warmed the day. The stream was there, too, waiting to numb my fingers blue and shock my face and drip down the back of my neck. I huddled close in my bag for one or two last moments of warmth and hoped that my friend was gone. This time it was different: the wish was the same, the reason for it was different— I even scolded myself for the selfish motives of the night before. If he was gone this morning, perhaps he had never been there in the night. Maybe he was some extraordinary manifestation of my will, my expectations, my dreams—even a manifestation of spirit independent of me.

I slid out of my bag and into my trousers before unzipping the tent flaps and crawling out into the morning. He wasn't there. I made a quick three-sixty: the stream to my right, Huarmihuañusca, the waterfall, Runkuracay, the jungle forest . . .

The Valley of the Rainbows was a valley of mist. If ever there was a setting out of myth, a place whence an apparition could come and return to, there it was before me. The dark green, tangled tropical forest that filled the sloping valley floor was shrouded in fog that seemed to rise from among the twisted vines and dripping leaves and fill every shadowed place. The cloying mists of the Pacamayo Valley: dense and unmoving over the trees; diaphanous and wispy at the edges where it clung to the steep walls of the ravine. I exhaled and watched the breath vapor hover there before me, and wondered if it was the breath of the jungle that I saw hovering over the Valley of the Rainbows. To my left the steep slope marked the progress of the Sun rising to the east—the shadow of Huarmihuañusca slid imperceptibly down the valley wall where the ruins of Runkuracay huddled just above the mist.

The fire had burned itself down to granite-colored ash, though a few embers still glowed faintly orange in the morning light and three or four separate wisps of smoke rose vertically in the still dawn air. Then I saw his rucksack. Just when I was about to consider the significance of his absence, I saw his pack beside a small boulder near the bank of the stream. I saw him lift his hand in greeting as he walked up the slight rise from the riverbank to the edge of our campsite. And then I felt the dull burn of the blister on the palm of my left hand, where I had burned it the night before.

7

I cannot tell how the truth may be;
I say the tale as 'twas said to me.

—*Sir Walter Scott*

IF I DWELL ON THE DETAILS OF MY MEETING WITH
the young man who accompanied me from the Pacamayo Valley to Machu
Picchu, it is because I cannot afford to be irresponsible in telling this story.
It is only by relating the events as they occurred and recreating the dialogue that we shared that I will be able to capture the essence of what happened, and ultimately what it all meant.

By the time we ate and broke camp and filled the canteens with coca
tea and buried the ashes of the fire, the Sun had found its way into the valley and the lingering mists were home to three rainbows: two distinctly
colored and well-defined, and one distant and vague. I will forever return to
that valley in my dreams and my meditations. Of all the things I have seen,
none comfort me as much as the view of Machu Picchu at dusk and the
Valley of the Rainbows just after dawn. It is reassuring to know that there
are places on this Earth both touched and untouched by humankind that
signify in perfect silence the enchantment of this world.

We left the valley and climbed a zig-zag path up the steep escarpment
ahead to the ruins of Runkuracay. Our way was paved: Stone steps were set
into the mountainside, and from here on the Royal Road of the Incas was
definitive.

We stopped at the ruins on the side of the hill, only to look back down at the Valley of the Three Rainbows and across to yesterday's pass. We wandered along the circular corridors formed by the curved granite walls of this curious outpost. There is a central courtyard, and there my young friend explained to me that the ruins were named by Hiram Bingham, who had undoubtedly asked his Quechua porters what this place was called. *Runkuracay,* they had replied, "Basket-Shaped Building". That was in 1915, four years after Bingham had "discovered" the lost city of Machu Picchu while searching for the fabled city of Vilcabamba, the last refuge of the Incas. He had returned to "discover" traces of the Inca Trail, including the stretch from the Pacamayo Valley to Puyupatamarca, the "Town in the Clouds," which waited for us at the end of the day's trek.

"We cannot know the original name of this place," said my friend. His voice came over my shoulder from where he stood in the center of the courtyard. From the top of the outer wall, I looked down into the valley— my last look, a bird's-eye view. "It was a place of rest, a *tambo* where travelers stopped on their way to the holy city." I jumped back down into the courtyard. "You believe that Machu Picchu was a religious center?" I asked, for I expected that his knowledge of Inca history was pragmatic. "Yes," he said. "But it is not Vilcabamba."

We left the ruins and continued our climb to the second pass, the pass named after the ruins. At 13,200 feet it would be a chore; but this trail was paved, my way was clear, and with yesterday's successful assault on Huarmihuañusca and a few hearty slugs of coca tea under my belt, I climbed with confidence, like Sir Edmund Hilary negotiating a flight of stairs. My companion kept up, matched my pace; he might have been my shadow for his constancy.

Vilcabamba is one of those gilt-edged, leather-bound legends that set your heart pounding and your imagination flying. The story of the search for Vilcabamba is the quintessential tale of the quest for a Lost City. Like Shambhala, Avalon, Atlantis, El Dorado, and Paititi, Vilcabamba is a place that lives in legend and has thrilled the hearts and stolen the lives of countless explorers over hundreds of years.

After the decisive slaughter at Sacsayhuaman in the spring of 1536, the defeated rebel Manco Inca fled Cuzco for the Urubamba Valley and his fortifications at Ollantaytambo; one hundred Spanish soldiers under the command of Hernando Pizarro followed close on his heels. Manco successfully repelled their attack; by diverting the river through irrigation canals, the Incas flooded the plains below the garrison and very nearly massacred the Spanish cavalry caught in the mire. Within the year the Spanish sent a force of three hundred against Ollantaytambo. Manco was outnumbered and fell back, retreating northwest through snowbound passes and into the Andean wilderness, where the Urubamba cut a canyon through a granite mountain range overwhelmed with dense, dripping jungle crawling with creatures the likes of which no Spaniard had ever seen. He crossed the foaming rapids of the river at a bridge slung between overhanging precipices, and disappeared into the valley of an affluent river to take refuge in his remote fortress city of Vitcos. Had the Spanish not stopped to sack Vitcos of its gold and women, Manco would have fallen there; but the Spaniards' lust for gold was greater than their lust for blood, and Manco escaped deeper into the wilderness, into the treacherous jungle fastness of the Andes known as Vilcabamba, the "Sacred Plain."

Vilcabamba, the "last refuge of the Incas," became a legend. From deep within the treacherous valleys and impregnable jungles of this place, Manco Inca would continue to lead the guerrilla rebellion that terrorized the Spanish settlers and inspired millions of Incas enslaved by the Spanish occupation.

In 1539 another of Francisco Pizarro's brothers, Gonzalo, lead one of the countless expeditions against Manco's notorious sanctuary; again and again the Spanish attempted to penetrate the labyrinth to the city in the jungle, where it was said that Manco had taken a great quantity of treasure, including "the largest and most valuable of the gold images of the sun which had been in the principal temple in Cuzco."

But Manco's palaces in the jungle were inviolate, and the approaches to the region made all the more inhospitable by the legions of native warriors who infested the province of Vilcabamba.

At this point in the story—for this was the story that entertained me as we climbed on toward the pass, Abra de Runkuracay, past the twin lakes with one name, Yanacocha, Black Lake—we stopped and caught our breath and wiped the sweat from our faces and refreshed ourselves with coca tea. I closed my eyes, and my imagination ran wild with morbid curiosity to the suffering of the tiny bands of Spanish mercenaries, unclean, long hair matted and tied in filthy braids under their crested metal helmets, faces stained with jungle rot and straining with the agony of *soroche,* altitude sickness, the body armor—the cuirasses that made them feel so invincible, but weighed them down like any false sense of security—dented and rusting with the sweat of the jungle that condensed on them; their hip-high leather boots caked with alluvial mud and slime; the swords—tempered in Toledo, now chipped and rusting like their armor—ready to put to death any traitorous native guide; scabbards that caught and tangled in the vines and branches that were everywhere too dense to see through. Their eyes mad with strain, hardship, gold . . .

After scores of attempts to rout the rebel Inca, the Spanish brought his wife, Cura Ocllo, to Ollantaytambo as a ransom for his surrender. They say that when Manco refused to negotiate with his wife's captors, Francisco Pizarro himself ordered that she be stripped, whipped, and like St. Sebastian, shot full of arrows. They say that her naked corpse was tied to a raft and dispatched down the Urubamba River that it might reach Vilcabamba.

"They say"—*dicen que,* "they say that"—how this simple phrase, *dicen que,* rings with romance and adventure and the unknown. The history of the Incas was an oral tradition spoken in *pukina,* the Inca tongue whose grammar was said to encode the secrets of their architecture and religion. Only the *quipucamayocs,* the artists who knew the cipher of the knotted *quipus* strands, knew the history and could repeat it; and *dicen que* seems to preface every morsel of the tale of the Inca Empire. I remember how the phrase punctuated our climb that morning and afternoon when we crested the pass of Runkuracay and descended, treading the fitted granite trail, to a spectacular view of a lush valley and, crowning a spur—a promontory jutting out into the valley—the ruins of Sayacmarca, "Inaccessible Town."

We continued our descent and then followed an abrupt flight of granite steps along the ridge of the spur to the ruins. Sayacmarca might have been built for strategic purposes; or its situation on the edge of a precipice— its commanding view of a verdant valley and the juncture of two Inca highways far below—could have been an aesthetic choice, a place for the Children of the Sun to rest and contemplate their world en route to the City of Light at Machu Picchu. Now it is a maze of monolithic walls flanking short stairways, baths fed by an aqueduct, and a triangular plaza on the edge of the cliff. We rested there, finished the three-day-old *quinoa* pancakes and dried fruit, dipped into the peanut butter, and drank tea.

And my companion continued his tale of the true Lost City of the Incas. The story of Vilcabamba is necessarily complicated—as any good legend is—by conflicting accounts. The chronicles that have survived were set down by such men as Pizarro's secretary, an Augustinian friar, a Spanish soldier of fortune, a Spanish nobleman and envoy of the Viceroy, and the Spanish son of an Inca princess. There are even the dictated memoirs of Titu Cusi, Manco's illegitimate son. All were written to serve the self-interests of the authors. Perhaps the oral tradition, the familiar story that was told to me that day, is a distillate of all accounts; it is certainly the way the legend lives.

They say that after Pizarro's assassination by a band of mutinous *conquistadores,* Manco was pleased to welcome seven of the outlawed Spanish conspirators at Vitcos. Vitcos was the threshold of the impenetrable Vilcabamba Range, and the royal chambers of this fortress city would act as the antechambers of the jungle kingdom beyond. Much of the drama of the next twenty-seven years would take place at Vitcos. It was there that Manco died in 1545, murdered by his seven Spanish guests in an ill-advised play for amnesty from the Spanish crown. Manco's son, Sayri Tupac, emerged from the sanctuary of Vilcabamba in 1557 and left the jungle by way of Vitcos to live the last four years of his life in Cuzco, where they say he was poisoned. Titu Cusi, Manco's illegitimate son, assumed the throne and launched a vicious campaign against the Spanish from Vilcabamba; and it was at Vitcos that the new Inca received instruction in Christianity from Father Diego Ortiz and dictated his memoir to Father Marcos Garcia. They say that these two friars may have been the only Spanish subjects to travel to the principal court of Vilcabamba, where they set about trying to convert the natives and where Father Diego would be accused of poisoning the young Inca in 1571. He was tortured for this and beaten to death and his body left to the condors, and his head undoubtedly joined those of the seven conspirators who killed Manco Inca: the seven rotting skulls that adorned the outer walls of the "palace" at Vitcos.

Father Diego's death was surely seen by the Spanish as a martyrdom; and when a viceregal ambassador was waylaid and killed en route to Vitcos, the Viceroy of King Philip II commanded an expeditionary force to penetrate the Cordillera de Vilcabamba and kill or capture the new Inca, Tupac Amaru. Of Manco Inca's three sons, Tupac Amaru was the least experienced in the art of war, and the Spanish expedition reached Vitcos and sacked the fortress there. But Tupac Amaru had fled deep into the jungle, down the rapids of the river, and the Spanish under Captain Garcia pursued him relentlessly, penetrating deeper into the fabled province than any that had gone before them.

They say that Tupac Amaru was found kneeling by a fire in the jungle. He was taken to Cuzco in chains. The last Inca lived long enough to return to the former capital, the jaguar-shaped city, and watch as his wife was publicly dismembered there. The last Son of the Sun was conscious long enough to be "converted" to Christianity and have his head cut off in the main square—in the belly of the Jaguar. That was in 1572, and that was the end of the greatest empire in the Western Hemisphere.

Unfortunately none of the chronicles of the conquest of Peru record the exact location of the fabled city in the jungle; many of the documents even confuse Vitcos for Vilcabamba itself. There is some evidence that the Spanish did in fact reach the "last refuge of the Incas"; but there are others who say (*dicen que*) the Spanish never found the Inca sanctuary and it was reclaimed by the jungle.

I could well imagine a city overwhelmed by the life of these valleys: Sayacmarca, the ruins at which we broke for lunch, was above it all—the dense growth of the lower regions where the mists of morning lingered. From the plaza at Sayacmarca, I looked up to the mountains that lay ahead of us to the northwest: the Inca Trail—a white granite-paved pathway cut into the shoulder of the green mountains—climbing steadily toward the pass above the ruins of Puyupatamarca. We left the ruins at midday and followed the perfectly preserved trail past a picturesque swamp called Ch'akicocha, Dry Lake, and up a long green incline, through a tunnel shaped out of a natural cleft in a rock face, across the mountainside, along the edge of ravines choked with tropical flora. There were butterflies, birds; the steady and sotto voce hum of insects filled the air, which I was accustomed to now; and I remember that afternoon as the finest I had ever spent in anyone's company but Antonio's.

The popular history of the search for Vilcabamba begins with Hiram Bingham, the Honolulu-born, Yale- and Harvard-educated gentleman explorer and author. In 1911 he established the location of Vitcos and explored the valleys of the Urubamba and the Cordillera de Vilcabamba in hopes of discovering the fabled last refuge of the Incas.

Bingham would discover ruins tangled in the primeval wilderness east of Vitcos at a place called Espiritu Pampa, the Plain of the Spirits. He would find traces of the Royal Road of the Incas and be the first to describe the ruins of Runkuracay, Sayacmarca, and countless others. But his most astonishing find would be to the west of Vitcos, where the Urubamba snakes around the base of two great pinnacles rising out of the valley basin. Machu Picchu, Bingham's celebrated "find," would go down in history as the Lost City of the Incas, for Bingham was convinced that at Machu Picchu he had found Vilcabamba.

Ironically he had found *a* lost city of the Incas, if not the fabled city that he sought. The discovery in the 1960s of the tangle of ruins that Bingham had glimpsed at Espiritu Pampa has lead archaeologists to conclude that Vilcabamba, the Sacred Plain and last refuge of the Incas, is in the wild country known as the Plain of the Spirits, fifty miles west of Machu Picchu.

"There are problems there now," said my friend. "The Sendero Luminoso, the guerrilla vigilantes, are there."

"So," I said, "the rebels strike out at the injustices and corruption of the modern Republic from the same hidden province where their ancestors once fought against Spain."

He smiled. "You have traveled in Peru, by foot. You have never had a problem?"

"No." There had certainly never been any problems in the 1970s, the years that I walked with Antonio, but the rural unrest in the Republic of Peru had yet to organize itself. Now they lurked in the mountain passes and in the jungle. I had seen them in the Amazon, heavily armed young men clothed in mismatched khaki and olive drab.

Subsequently I have always felt their presence, always knew that they were there, aware of my movements and of my work. "No," I said, "I have never had a problem. The Sendero know my work by now, and I usually travel with men who are known to them as healers."

We made the third and final pass as the sun was setting over Salcantay, the grandfather of the *apus,* at 20,565 feet. I stood at over 13,000 feet and opened my eyes wide to the ravines that cleaved the highlands before me; from that high place the jungle growth that carpeted the mountainsides looked like moss. The towering, snowcapped *apus,* now touched by the Sun's setting rays, glowed as though lit from within; like the clouds that settled around them, they captured and shone back to me the final light of the day. Down the hill at my feet the granite ruins of Puyupatamarca, "Town in the Clouds," were wrapped in the shade of dusk.

After the Sun had disappeared behind the mountains, and the moon —one day shy of full—had transformed all the glacial peaks from gold to silver, we sat by the fire and watched the stars appearing over the crisp horizon and beginning their transit of this hemisphere; and for a moment I sensed that it was the Earth that was moving, turning in the heavens. Although I sat cross-legged on a hill, I was miles above the surface of the sea and I could have been free-floating, suspended in space and watching the Earth turn; I could almost hear it moving.

"There is a story that I heard as a child, I think, because I have always known it," said my friend without looking at me. My eyes were fixed on the jagged horizon, his on the moon.

El Sol lloró de alegría, he said. "The Sun wept with joy." *Y una lagrima de fuego cayó sobre la barriga fértil de la Pachamama.* "And a tear of fire fell upon the pregnant belly of the Earth . . ."

It sounded like a children's story, the way he told it. It was the same story that I had begun in Canyon de Chelly, the story that I had made up until it had acquired a life of its own. Some stories are like that, and the place and the time and the nature of my work that night in Arizona had conspired to form the story, the first story ever told: the story that was created spontaneously; every time it is told is the first time . . .

Y el Pueblo de Piedra . . . "And the People of the Stones gathered around the great tear . . ."

It had everything: the courtship of the Earth and Sun, and the Moon as sister and midwife . . . even the Stone People. I wish I could have seen myself that night, hanging on every word of his simple story; the same story, told with the sing-song cadence of a fairy tale.

Y ahi ardió como una estrella caida . . . "And there it burned like a fallen star. But the People of the Stones could not contain the great tear, and the fire spread over the surface of the Earth. And in the valleys, and along the rivers it traveled, finding its way down, deep into the bosom of the Earth where it would burn for a very long time . . ."

It sounded like a fable recited in a nursery.

He sat there by the fire with his legs drawn up, his hands clasped, his elbows resting on his knees. Sometimes he lifted his head to look at the silver-toned valley below, the fire, my face.

Y la Tierra tembló . . . "And the Earth trembled when life was born. And soon man emerged from the sea at the top of the world; the Children of the Sun rose from the waters of their mother, the Earth. And on the ground and in the cracks of the rocks and in the valleys and along the rivers where the great tear had traveled and cooled, they would find something soft that shone like the Sun, and this was gold," he said, and I watched him say it.

"And also they would find other stones who remembered when the Sun shed its tear, and with these stones the Children of the Sun and the Earth could make fire and warm themselves when the Earth turned her face into the shadows of night. Fire was the gift of a proud father to his children, and his children would live in his golden light and raise their eyes to him in thanks. And the Sun and the Earth would go on making life, for they are very passionate. And the Children of the Sun and the Earth would love their mother and worship their father and live in the paradise that their parents had made for them.

"The gold was a remembrance of the Sun's ancient love for the Earth. The gold was of the Earth, and it looked like the Sun, and the Children of the Sun who lived *here*—" he raised his eyes to look at the moonlight-bathed peaks that made the horizon—"gathered the gold from the ground and used it to cover their places of worship and to fashion their sacred ornaments.

"But there were others who coveted the product of the Sun's love—not because of its beauty, but because of its rareness. These others also were Children of the Sun, but they did not call themselves Children of the Sun; they called themselves the children of a god. They came here to claim this land and its gold for themselves and their father, and the Children of the Sun took what was left of the Sun's ancient love for the Earth and went to a place called Vilcabamba. And there they disappeared.

"And that is how fire and gold came to the Earth and how men have used them. And that is why they say, *dicen que,* that the Gold of the Incas is at Vilcabamba.

I asked him where he had heard this story. He claimed that he had always known it. The perfect answer. He said that it is a very old story. "I know," I said. "I have told it."

We could have discussed it then, talked about my experience in Canyon de Chelly—making up this same story as an exercise in accessing what? Genetic memory? Ancestral memory? Something that can be *told* but not *known*? But we didn't because I felt uneasy. I thanked him for the story, and said something about how wonderful were the "old stories," something about how well he told it, and now I'm in my tent, in my sleeping bag, with my flashlight hanging from the tent struts, writing this all down and feeling as though I am writing in a dream.

8

What beck'ning ghost, along the moon-light shade
Invites my steps, and points to yonder glade?

—*Alexander Pope*

I ROSE TO A LAND OF MIST. I WOKE EARLY THE NEXT
morning and unzipped myself from my tent and dressed in the cold haze—
a dewy vapor that clung to my face and bare chest. Our cloud-level campsite
was thick with it. The nylon surface of my tent was granulated with tiny
frozen beads of condensation. I flicked the taut fabric with my middle finger, and the beads bounced and slid to the ground. I emptied a canteen of
pure water into the pot and set it to boil for coffee, then walked to the
downslope of the hill and peered through the drizzle at the ruins below. I
could just make them out: the walls, semi-intact buildings, stairways, the
rows of ritual baths, the flights of terraces that fall away down the hill—a
granite-walled city looming in the fog of an Andean dawn.

My friend was down there, somewhere. Once again he had politely refused my offer to share the tent. He had spent the night in the ruins.
Wondering how he had fared in the cold, I struck the tent and packed everything but the breakfast food. Water is slow to boil at altitude, so I pulled
my alpaca sweater over my head and squatted by the Primus and tried to
warm my hands in the steam rising from the water. I imagined his night,
remembered the countless long-ago evenings I have spent in the half-shelter
of ruins and shallow caves where the darkness is silent in attendance to the

sounds and sensations that play in the mind. I wrote in my journal. The writing is cramped and stiff with the finger-numbing cold.

The outlines of rooms, great roofless halls of fitted speckled granite. Temples, observation posts, settlements engineered a thousand years ago, built to last an eternity. Enigmas now, all of them: Sacsayhuaman, Corihuayrachina, Sayacmarca, Puyupatamarca, Machu Picchu, Vitcos . . . Vilcabamba? Vestiges of the spirit, the soul, the *mind* of a people who inhabited this place on Earth. And I wander over the contours of this land, its convolutions and invaginations, and observe all these clues, and I have found that there is a way of inhabiting these spaces and experiencing them.

When the water was boiling, I slipped the journal into its zipper compartment, made coffee, and started to hum something. All of it—every moment of that morning—was a conscious attempt to distract myself from the sensation that I awoke with. It was a familiar feeling, a feeling that something had happened or was about to, a feeling that had accompanied me through so many experiences that I had come to respect it and to be wary of its effect. All that had happened was that a hiker I had met on the Inca Trail had told me a story that I had told—or one that had told itself to me. There was nothing to be made of this, and the coincidence was not in itself responsible for the subtle anxiety that I felt. I would do what I could to make this a normal day.

By the time the morning mists had cleared, we were on our way. We were descending slightly, traversing a mountainside, the left side of the Urubamba Valley—tropical forest again: vines, moss, tree ferns, palms, cedar trees. The clouds were still low, sealing off the valley from the sky. He had, it seems, slept well in one of the semicircular stone-walled rooms that faced the valley on the edge of the ruins. He had bathed in one of the spring-fed ritual baths.

"It was very peaceful," he said.

"Did you dream?"

He smiled. "No," he said. "You believe these places are very significant." It was a blank statement, a fact; he said it like a director telling an actor something about the character he is playing.

So I told him my story: how I had come to Peru to study the effects of the *ayahuasca* and had discovered a tradition of psychology that was unknown to the Western world—a tradition that had been preserved by his ancestors. I described the Medicine Wheel, the mythic journey of the Four Winds, and elaborated on its elegance while we walked side-by-side along the over-grown trail.

"It is a psychology of the sacred," I said. "It is a tradition that identifies the Divine as a naturally occurring phenomenon—that is to say that the Divine is in Nature—and it is by accessing the state of consciousness that informs life that we gain the wisdom we require to change, to evolve." He was listening carefully; at least I seemed to have his attention. He matched my pace and when the trail narrowed he would let me go ahead so that I never spoke to his back.

"In my culture," I said, "the idea of accessing Divine consciousness directly is a blasphemy. But the rudiments of the Medicine Wheel have survived here—your people have secretly maintained a tradition and practice that is as old as our species itself. It has survived evolution; it has survived plagues, pestilence, and wars—the Conquest. I think that it is based on an ancient memory of a state of mind that was *pre*conscious—a state of mind that existed before we acquired the ability to *reason*. It was never displaced by reason, not complemented by it. Do you understand?"

"It seems very reasonable," he said. He was a very clever young man.

"The Medicine Wheel describes the journey," I said.

"In the South I shed my past like the serpent sheds its skin. I enter a state of consciousness—a realm of awareness within which the most significant events and people of my past are manifest before me. It is in this state of mind that I am able to reexperience the impact of these events and people, to see and feel them for what they were, and essentially to dismiss them one by one—to free myself from their grip."

By this time I was breathless with exertion and raw enthusiasm. Rarely had the process of the Medicine Wheel so effortlessly described itself. Maybe it was because I had personalized it.

"In the West I confront fear. Fear lives in the future, and our greatest fear is death. We fear what we do not know, and by experiencing death we learn to maintain awareness and identity after death. If I am able to experience myself as a being of conscious energy—as a Child of the Sun—then death becomes a doorway only; it loses its menace. It is a phase of an infinite lifetime."

"You know this," he said.

"Yes."

"You know this, or you *suspect* this?"

I stopped and unhooked my canteen from my belt. He waved off the drink I offered him and I took a long pull at the bottle. I would never see this man again. Why should I be dishonest? "I have experienced it. I believe it," I said.

"You took *ayahuasca?*"

"Yes."

"And you experienced death?"

"Yes. I saw my own body decay before my eyes. I felt the loss of each sensation as it passed."

He nodded. "But you knew that you would come back."

I shook my head. "No, I didn't. I didn't think about it. I wasn't aware that . . . " I stopped because I remembered the fear. I know that my experiences in the jungle so many years ago had freed me to live a life of profound and even reckless experience because I had felt death and knew that it was safe. But I had felt the fear and, yes, I had known somehow, somewhere in that long night in Ramón's hut, that I would come back, that Ramón would bring me back.

"Go on," he said.

"By honoring my past—freeing myself from its hold on my present, and by confronting death—learning that I will leave this world alive, I have acquired the ability to live fully in the present. I am not boasting, I am using myself as an example—"

"I understand."

"I have learned," I said, "something fundamental about my existence. I have learned that the body is a vessel of consciousness and that I do not have only seventy-odd years to live. I have, therefore, a new relationship with the Earth. I have become a steward of the Earth, for it might be my home for longer than anyone can count. And like the cat that represents the West, I know that I have many lives to live within this lifetime. I have lived several of them already—stages in my life. The work of the West has taught me to leap gracefully from one life to the next without clinging to the people or the events that influenced it.

"Next is the North, where I journey to acquire the wisdom of all those who have journeyed before me. This is the most difficult leg to describe of the journey of the Four Winds. The ability to access a vast sea of information, of knowledge and wisdom, is somehow automatic. It is a state of consciousness that I have only glimpsed. This is a realm of personal mastery that I do not yet fully understand. I sometimes think that I carry a wisdom with me that I am not aware of—a wisdom that is not the product of my own experiences. I know that I can inhabit a place—Machu Picchu, for instance—and know things about it, about its purpose as a religious center, a place of initiation. But this is all very vague."

"Yes," he said.

"Somewhere I acquired prescient skills—I can feel events of the future and often sense the past of a person or even a place. I know when there will be an earthquake, and I am sensitive to the moods—the joys and traumas—of those whom I love even when I am separated from them by thousands of miles. I feel presences—forms that are, I think, manifestations of human and Nature energies, both positive and negative forces. But these things are all incidental skills. I don't fully understand the North because it is not something that is understood; it is experienced, and my experiences there are limited. But you can see that it is inaccessible to any who seek it encumbered by preconceptions or fears—the past or the future."

"Yes."

"And then there is the East, which is said to be the most difficult journey. In the East I learn to reconcile all that I know with the world in which I live. The East is the return home. I have adapted the journey of the Four Winds into my practice of psychology; I have described my own experiences as I had them . . ."

"So that is your work of the East?" he asked.

"Yes," I admitted. "That and the work I do with individuals and groups. I have brought hundreds of people to Peru to work in these places."

"To the ruins?"

"Yes. They *are* significant, you see. Some of them have always been sacred places—places that lend themselves to meditation and transformation—like an archetypal landscape, the landscape of a dream, a place that inspires awe and reminds us somehow of an ancient memory or simply sings to our unconscious." He gave me that look, that peculiar and characteristic expression of assessment that I had first seen the night we met.

"Besides," I said, "learning shamanic skills in Machu Picchu is like learning how to compose chamber music in Salzburg."

He grinned.

Suddenly we were zig-zagging down a steep hillside of scrub. Bingham had never made it this far; the Inca Trail in 1915 was impassable shortly beyond Puyupatamarca and the ruins of Wiñay Wayna—the towers and plazas, ritual baths, and fantastic flights of stairs set into the cliff side that falls to the banks of the Urubamba—were not discovered until the 1940s; it was midday when we discovered them.

We had descended a thousand feet from Puyupatamarca, and the overcast had turned gray and menacing. I was anxious to reach Machu Picchu by nightfall, anxious to show off to my companion the abandoned city that I knew so intimately. I had evidently engaged his attention with my description of his Inca heritage. So we bypassed the ruins without a word. Half a mile later he said:

"You believe in what you teach."

It had the tone of a serious question, and I answered as genuinely as I could manage. "Yes. I believe in what I have learned from my own experiences."

"What else?"

I almost told him about the Medicine Wheel and the response systems of the limbic brain—but it did not seem to matter at the time. It seemed then like just another unprovable hypothesis—a diverting suggestion that I had used to bridge the gap between my work and my Western training. Not that there is anything wrong with the idea; I believe it still, but it is like an explication of a poem—the more you explain it in terms other than its own, the less it enchants.

"What else do you believe in?"

I had heard him the first time. I said: "I believe that psychology is like physics—like quantum theory; I believe that the act of studying the psyche alters it."

"What else?"

He should have been satisfied. Maybe he wasn't really listening, so I said the first thing that came to mind: "I believe that the realms of consciousness are regions of the human mind that are as mapable as any terrain. There is a topography to them that can be described."

We walked in silence for a long while.

That was the gist of our dialogue; I remember what was said, if not how I said it. The feeling of renewed enthusiasm, of a purpose recaptured that day, stayed with me through the night and is with me still; the words themselves were left along the trail behind us, and all I have done is to recollect them to recreate the essence of that day because I know now how important it was to me later.

It was late in a gray afternoon that threatened to break and never did. A steep flight of Inca steps suddenly rose up before us; it lead up a densely overgrown forest slope. We climbed without stopping; I had caught my third wind—my body had shifted into a new gear, a rare rate of respiration and function—my system had adapted to an exhilarated state, and nothing could stop me. On the top step I flexed my hand, fanned out my fingers, and watched it tremble. I took off my hat and walked along the ridge—a cleft between two valleys—to a shaded spot all cushioned with fallen leaves, where a monolithic gateway of lichen-stained granite has stood for five or six or seven hundred years. This is the Intipunku, the Gateway of the Sun, the entrance to Machu Picchu.

We stopped in the shade, paused before passing through. Ahead the trail traced a gentle arc, following the green-forested hillside that curved away to the right, and I knew that we would see the city below and to the right as soon as we passed through the gate. "And what do *you* believe in?" I asked him, suddenly.

He looked at me, then past me—through the gate to the green hillside. "I believe that we are Children of the Sun," he said. "And if we are Children of the Sun, we will grow to be like the Sun. We are here—" he looked around, left, right, down at the ground and back into my eyes—"to become gods."

It has often been noted that a peculiarity of Machu Picchu and Huayna Picchu—the twin peaks of the same pinnacle that rises out of a bowllike depression in the Urubamba Valley—is that they seem to be perpetually in sunshine. When we passed through the Intipunku, we passed from one valley to another, and the Inca City of Light was glowing in the sunbeams of late afternoon. Behind us all was overcast and dour, and below us now the shadows were sharp, the colors warmed in the Sun.

Machu Picchu was as it always is in my imagination: a living city of empty buildings, a multileveled maze of speckled granite walls, a teaming complex of plazas and courtyards and flagstoned promenades and proud temples and grand terraces in the slanting rays of a setting Sun.

As we walked along the trail that follows the hillside and curves in toward the knoll where the Death Stone sits beside a thatched-roof watchman's hut, I noticed that he looked at the ruins with an expression that was almost wistful—as though he was seeing something through a window, something that he wanted but could not touch. Maybe, I thought, it was his heritage that he saw.

The Sacred City known as Machu Picchu affects people in different ways, but it always affects them. Its effect on me has changed over the years that I have come to know it so well. When I was young and full of the romance of early adventures, it was a fossilized citadel, an aerie of pre-Columbian culture nestled on a saddle ridge and clouded by mystery. It soon became a personal landmark—the place where my past had become visible to me and where I had experienced a profound catharsis. Then it was a place of teaching, a stage where I tested my skills in directing subtle dramas of personal transformation, where I tried to effect shifts in people's perceptions of themselves and their world. Recently it had become a place of meditation, a place my mind would fly to and wander through when I was far away and troubled.

We descended to the top of the knoll and I led the way to the Death Stone, a beamy block of gray granite carved in the shape of a fat canoe, floating in the long green grass and yellow wildflowers.

I sloughed off my pack and looked down the hill and into the city, where a guide was leading one of the last two groups of tourists down a long, narrow flight of stairs and across a dry moat and toward the terraces that lead to the main entrance by the caretakers' houses below us and to the right.

Often I had laid myself down on this stone, where my energy body would be disengaged in a symbolic ritual of death; the stone was fashioned as a vehicle for delivering the spirit from the West, the region of silence and death, so that it might return from the East where the Sun rises and life is born. Following this elegant and simple ritual, the individual is able to enter the city as one who has already died, as a Child of the Sun.

I offered to perform this symbolic service for my young friend, and was curious about how he would respond. We would avoid the guards, I explained—I knew a place where we could go and wait until dark—and I would take him on a nighttime tour of the sacred city of his ancestors. Tonight Machu Picchu would glisten in the light of a full moon that would show off the ruins to their best advantage. Now I explained the significance of the Death Stone and he listened, expressionless.

"No," he said. "Thank you."

He turned away and looked left, away from the city, down the hill and across a flight of terraces to where the sheer mountainside curved around and out of sight. I knew the trail that led there. It becomes narrow and treacherous, unstable as it skirts the very edge of the mountainside and all but disappears in a hopeless tangle of overgrowth. Eventually it ends beside a naked cliff of red rock crisscrossed with hanging vines as thick as an arm, and there is a broken bridge, an Inca suspension bridge that hangs against the rock wall just out of reach. I have stood hanging onto a bush and leaning out over that precipice and figuring my chances of clinging to that rock face long enough to reach the wrecked bridge that would surely collapse under my weight. That was where his gaze led—it was across the terraces and a dizzying half-hour walk around the bend of the mountainside.

"And thank you for walking with me," he said. Then he told me that he was leaving—rather, that he was not stopping here. "I am going on," I think he said, simply. The news was so unexpected, and delivered so matter-of-factly, that I just looked at him. He smiled back at me and hiked his rucksack higher up on his shoulders. He said something about how late it was and how interesting our conversations had been.

There was nothing I could do. I am not sure that there was anything I *wanted* to do. Truth be told, his presence had been something of an imposition and a distraction from my intended solo trek, although by telling him so much of my past and my passions I had returned to Machu Picchu filled with enthusiasm. And there was the story that he had told, that first story. I wanted to talk to him about that, say something about the story that we had unwittingly shared; I would have brought it up that night—it would have been an appropriate way to while away the time until the watchmen made their final sweep of the ruins and headed back to the caretakers' houses.

But it was not going to happen that way. Things had been askew ever since I touched down in Lima. So I just looked at him for the last time: his poncho and workman's boots and rucksack—his wide open Indian face and purposeful eyes and straight black hair.

We spoke for a moment, and then he said something that I have reason never to forget. And before I could warn him about the dangers of the trail and the sagging bridge and the gorge that fell to the rapids, he was off in the other direction. He headed down the hill and crossed the dry moat and followed the steps down to the central courtyard and off down the center of the wide flat plaza that runs the length of the city. I watched him go—past the temples and chambers and semiexcavated walls and stairways and terraces—toward the meadow where the Pachamama Stone marks the edge of the city. He turned left before reaching the meadow; he disappeared over the edge of the city at a place where I knew there were terraces, and below them a way down the mountain, though it is unmarked.

I wondered if I had heard him correctly.

"Where are you going?" I had asked him.

And he had said: "I am going to Vilcabamba."

9

The eye of man hath not heard, the ear of man hath not seen,
man's hand is not able to taste, his tongue to conceive,
nor his heart to report, what my dream was.

—*Shakespeare*

I SKIRTED THE RUINS BY A FAVORITE ROUTE. I descended the hill and used the terraces like a flight of giant stairs; like Gulliver in the land of the Brobdingnagians, I jumped down from one six-foot step to the next until I reached the bottom, the side of the hill that fell away just below the outer walls of the southwest sector. I made my way clockwise around the ruins, stumbling through the rock quarry and striding confidently along the length of the terraces below the Main Temple and the Intihuatana—the walled-in carved rock known as the "hitching post of the Sun"—then scrambling up another flight of short terraces to the northern end of the long central plaza. At that point I was near the spot where my friend had disappeared over the edge of the hill, and I looked down along 2,000 vertical feet of russet brown soil and gray rubble, *chilca* bushes and pigweed and dry grass, to the bend in the white roiling rapids of the Urubamba. He was long gone.

I crouched behind the riser of the highest terrace—the one level with the broad plaza—and looked for the watchman. I waited patiently, for there were a hundred corners that he could have appeared around as he patrolled through the ruins at a pace learned to match the rate of the approaching darkness. I had just started to move—to boost myself up over the ledge—when I saw him emerge from the ruin group near the Temple of the Condor in the southeast sector and stroll away toward the ritual baths and the stairway that leads toward the dry moat and back to his station on the hill across from the Death Stone. I glanced to my left—to the meadow of the Pachamama Stone—as I crossed the plaza and hoisted myself up into a group of ruined buildings in the northeast sector. I scaled an easy wall, straddled it, then dropped down on the other side and I was invisible, protected from view beside a little tree that grew in a half-excavated fold of broken-down wall.

Whether they are superstitious or have simply come to respect the dark magic of the city, the watchmen generally avoid the ruins between sunset and sunrise, choosing to take up their stations in huts on the outside—as far from the center of town as possible—where they can conduct their surveillance from a safe distance. Staying in the ruins after dark is strictly forbidden; and although I have come to know the watchmen, the archaeologists, and the various government officials who guard, study, and administer the "Lost City of the Incas," and although they know me and have permitted me to conduct workshops in the night—and have even participated in a few of those nocturnal exercises—I am careful never to take advantage of the relationship. Now, alone, I was particularly anxious to arrive unnoticed. I had no doubt that I would see them in the morning. We would have coffee and talk about the most recent finds and they would ask how the night passed.

Out of sight in my little granite cove, I ate what was left of my rations—some nuts and nut crumbs and the hard heel of sausage and the last of my peanut butter scraped from its jar with a dry-cracked and folded *quinoa* pancake. Tomorrow I would wander down the hill to the river and eat at the train station and catch the train back to Cuzco, but tonight I contented myself with polishing off my stores and saving only enough water to get me through the night. And the night was upon me. It was good that I was alone, grand that I had made this trip: reviewed so much of my past, renewed so much of my fervor, worked the kinks out of my body and mind. I had even lost a little weight; I scooted down to rest my head against my pack and my trousers slid up my waist. I folded my arms across my chest, and knowing somehow that I would connect with Antonio this night, closed my eyes and nodded off.

I dozed fitfully. I needed rest and I needed my wits.

I knew that I was exhausted from the day's hike, but knowing that I was here with a purpose and could not afford to miss this full moon had me waking every fifteen minutes to stare at the luminous dial of my watch. This went on interminably because I was too tired not to try for another hour's rest and too wound up to let myself go. Finally I rinsed the grogginess from my face with water and drained the last of the tea from my other canteen; and leaving my pack by the tree, climbed over the wall and lowered myself down into the central plaza.

The city was splendid in the moonlight. The moon was a perfect orb shining brazen white in the charcoal black sky above a bank of clouds that still loomed over the next valley. There was the hint of moisture in the air, and the air was moving east to west. Already the Intipunku was obscured by fog—in the night it was as though the trail by which we had come and the mountain it ran across had dissolved into the night. But although the weather was encroaching on the city, still there was star-pricked black sky above; the grassy plaza that ran the length of the city was gray-green, and the walls and temples and stairways of granite shone like tarnished silver.

Had I not known the nature of this place, and had I not come to intimate terms with the night and all the possibilities the darkness holds— the demons it harbors like criminals, and the spirits to whom night is day—then I would never have moved from my little niche. We *are* Children of the Sun, and we live in his splendor and rely on his light to see with our own two eyes. And what we see with our own two eyes are the boundaries of our world. We see what is up and what is down, and orient ourselves by the light of the Sun or imitations of it. But take away the light and we are helplessly dependent on our lesser senses. In the night the boundaries become indistinct and our senses are on the alert; we are insecure because we have never learned to trust anything that we don't see with our own two eyes. So fear lives in the night, too.

I have developed a close relationship with the night. In forty years— half of it spent chasing after the things that we know the least of, things that live outside of the range of our own two eyes—I have become accustomed to the darkness and, at least, patient with myself alone in the night.

So the eeriness was familiar. I summoned up my tolerance for it and wandered north toward the edge of the ruins, toward the massive shape of Huayna Picchu, Young Peak, also called Grandmother Peak, looming in the silver-toned darkness, rising hundreds of feet above the ruins, presiding over them in eternal attendance.

The Pachamama Stone is an upended slab of granite twenty feet long and ten high that stands in a meadow at the edge of the ruins and near the narrow ridge that leads to Huayna Picchu. The face of the stone is lichen-blotched speckled granite and as smooth and precisely cut as its upper edge is irregular and evidently untouched, although its silhouette matches that of the distant horizon—the skyline of the mountains beyond. This is the place of the Mother Earth, Pachamama, and it was here that I had spent a long-ago night flat on my back in the meadow and felt the prostrate figure of an Indian maiden lay herself down within me, and I had gone down, into the Earth, and seen the most wonderful things. She had left me then; and she was at once an old Indian crone—hideous old yellow-toothed wrinkled relic of a woman—and virginal maiden, and she had disappeared as she walked away through the grass toward the stone. She might have stepped into it. It had been an experience that lasted all night, and all night a friend had witnessed our tryst from the shelter of a thatched-roof stone hut on the edge of the clearing.

I had thought at the time that my experience had been an archetypal brush with the realms of the North: the place of wisdom, and the place identified by shamanic lore as the domain of the feminine. There are legends that speak of Huayna Picchu as a hollow mountain, a great honeycombed labyrinth of a place where an old crone lived. This was the mistress of the mountain. She was a hundred years old and lived deep within the hollow core of the mountain, fed by the energy of the Earth that coursed through the tunnels and passageways like the mineral springs she drank from. There were said to be places where the light of the Sun entered the mountain, and there were great disks of polished gold that bent and focused the light this way and that to illuminate her home. She was a shaman, at once the spirit and the caretaker of the mountain in which she dwelled.

And the Pachamama Stone was the gateway to the mountain, and my friend had been so encouraged by the marvel that he had witnessed that he was sure that I had been loved by the spirit of Huayna Picchu. I have never been sure of anything but the experience and the lessons of personal ecology that I learned subliminally during my descent into the Earth.

That was a fond memory of long ago—a story already told. This night as I stood in the center of the meadow in the moonlight and faced the stone, I felt only the contentment of having come this far to return to a favorite place. I was alone; something had called me to make this journey, and I was determined to serve every moment of my time with as little expectation and as much skill as I could muster.

So I stood in the center of the meadow and invoked the spirits of the Four Winds. My salutation to the elemental spirits of Nature has become embellished over the years; I have elaborated on the four directions and improvised on its imagery in ways calculated to engage people's attention and imagination. On this night, alone in the meadow and feeling sentimental, I found myself repeating the salutation that Antonio had taught me on the occasion of our first work together: a simple and dramatic prayer to Nature.

I turned to the south and called upon the Serpent of the South, Sachamama, to wrap herself around me, to fold me in her great coils of light. I faced the west and called upon Mother-Sister Jaguar, the golden jaguar that has seen the birth and death of galaxies, in its lithesome grace to circle the meadow and to watch over me. I summoned the wisdom of the North, the place of the ancient ones; I called upon the grandmothers and grandfathers to receive me, to welcome me, to allow me to sit in council with them. Facing east I called upon the Eagle to come to me from its mountaintop, to teach me with its eyes, that my vision might penetrate the Earth and the heavens; to soar with me, that I might fly wing to wing with the Great Spirit. I knelt and touched the soil beside a little tuft of grass and intoned my prayer to the Pachamama, Mother Earth who fed me and nurtured me at her breast, that she might teach me how to walk on her belly with beauty and grace. I lifted my face to the infinite blackness between two stars above me and saluted the Sun and Viracocha, the Great Spirit. I testified that all that I do is in honor of my Mother Earth, and Father Sun.

And then I sat cross-legged in the center of the meadow and closed my eyes and willed myself into a restful state.

My invocation, the prayer that I had offered to the winds, had, I am sure, summoned my will and focused my intent and defined my purpose: to free my perception so that I could inhabit this favorite place for a time and let it sing to me. I listened.

That a place can have a vibration of its own is a fancy that has found its only acceptance and expression by poets who have bent every rule of reason to describe metaphorically the effect on a human psyche of a cathedral or a place in the woods or a pile of rocks on a headland. And it is peculiar of the clinical thinkers that they too might read such descriptions and acknowledge such sentiments—like any of us, they have found themselves *feeling* for no apparent reason when visiting a place that has a history, whether personal or popular—but because the cause is invisible and cannot be measured, such experiences are discounted.

What happened to me in the meadow that night was not solely the result of my personal preparation nor the effect of the magic that resides in this place. From a shamanic perspective preparation is internal *and* external; one must have the personal power to summon the power that sleeps in the stones. Simply, like a stringed instrument vibrating of its own accord to the music of the orchestra that surrounds it, I responded to what was present. The place sang to me again.

It begins when I least expect it. I sit there and focus my awareness up into my forehead, that third eye that has seen so much more than the other two. I breathe steadily from my stomach and open myself to the place in the night; and when I suck the saliva from the inside of my cheeks and gums and swallow, I taste the residual bitterness of the coca tea. When I touch the soil I can feel its coolness and the dirt that clings to my fingers as I lift them away. When I inhale I smell burning rosemary and sweet grass; the moisture in the air is seasoned with sweet-smelling herbs. When I listen I hear the rattle and hum of a subtle rhythm; when I look I see young men and women, forms fitted with native finery, beaded waist ornaments with weighted leather thongs flapping, ankle bracelets of dried seedpods or hollow nutshells clonking at the ends of bare legs shining brown in the crackling light of a fire snapping and sparking in a stone brazier that is like a giant granite mortar there in the meadow. There are six . . . seven . . . eight . . .? I lose track counting as they move, dancing in a slow circle around the fire. Some wear ponchos or long, loose-sleeved shirts of thick and richly embroidered fabric dyed yellow and black and orange and red; and there are breastplates of gold polished with lime juice—I know this somehow—and bracelets and gold bands above some elbows. They are not barefoot. I notice soft leather sandals, the leather gathered and tied below the ankle. There are gold headbands so thin they are flush to the foreheads of the women. And there are frills of jungle feathers, mantles of green and red and yellow and brown. Clockwise, the men and women move around the fire and throw offerings of wildflowers and tiny folded bundles of weeds and herbs into the only source of light here—this fire that casts fantastic moving shadows against the surface of the Pachamama Stone.

It is hours—one, maybe two—since I began my meditation here, and what has manifest is something grand, something that I know that I am part of as I breathe in the sweet, pungent incense and feel the water that sprinkles my forehead and face. A young girl with black hair, plaited and woven with ribbons, walks counterclockwise, and dips her small hand into a ceramic bowl. She waves her hand in an unpracticed manner, snapping her wrist, and the water flicks from the ends of her perfect small fingers in a blessing of the dancers and of me. I watch her move contrary to the rest of them; she is shy, and the dancers laugh and smile at her shyness.

It is raining now, too, a light spattering of rain. I am entranced by the jogging two-step, half-step, two-step of the dancers, and the hearty hollow clatter of rattling nutshells and seedpods, seduced by the rattle and hum of the rhythm and the wide smiling faces and the glint of gold and the snapping and popping of the fire and the smell of rosemary.

I am being taken by the experience and I am willing to let myself go, although I feel for one involuntary shivering instant that I will never step out of the circle, that I will never wake from this state—that is how I know that I am being taken by it. On my feet now, moving with the circle around the fire, the step is easy, effortless to follow, and around I go until I stand outside the circle, at the edge of the Pachamama Stone; and the dance continues as the rain falls and I follow the lead of the little girl with the plaited hair. She wears a white *manta* cloth dress given shape by the woven patterned belt around her tiny waist. She walks ahead as the sounds of the dance and the seedpods and nutshells and the humming grow faint—doubtless they echo off the meadow face of the Pachamama Stone, and we are on the other side of the great stone, walking away in the moonlight following a dirt path across the narrow saddle ridge to Huayna Picchu. I wish that I could remember the purpose of the ceremony that I left behind, but I never knew it.

There is no light but the moonlight that colors everything gray, everything but the little dress that glows silver-white and moves ahead of me. My gaze is transfixed by its seemingly disembodied motion, so that at first I am aware that I am climbing only because I am following the glowing dress and it is moving up steadily and ahead of me. Then I look down, and I can make out my boots following the groove in the overgrown hillside that is the trail that rises relentlessly, vertically, leaving no margin for error. I know that in daylight the path that leads to the granite peak of Huayna Picchu is a challenge that is sometimes met on all fours; it is a path that is scaled rather than walked, and it is a fearsome thing in the night. I cannot see where it leads but up. Up, and the shape, the white figure that I followed, is gone, no longer above me against the tangled outline of the solid black mass of the mountain. I am alone in the darkness and there is nothing but the smell of the mud and the feel of the wet branch that I hold to steady myself on the sharp incline, and the soft, sibilant sound of the rain falling on the mountain and on the ruins of Machu Picchu, now so far below me. I realize that I have been climbing without pause for a long time and I am two-thirds of the way to the peak. I cannot go back, and the way down is too hazardous; so I go up, forever.

And then I am clinging to the slick and undulating surface of a granite slab of stone set into the mountain face and follow the path, which is V-shaped, a channel between adjacent boulders, until I am surrounded by hard, wet granite, and I remember that there is a passageway, a natural tunnel here somewhere, two-thirds of the way to the top, and yes, I can see the slanted slitlike opening ahead of me in the dark wet grayness of the night, and I am soon edging my way through, stooped and leaning all at once to squeeze my way along this ridiculous passageway through the stone until I am out the other end in a flat place. The top of the peak is a jumble of megalithic slabs rising up before me.

All at once I see her. She is no longer above me. She is motionless to my right, standing behind a boulder protruding from the mountainside. She moves on out of sight and I follow, over the rock, and I am on the pathless cliff side. I turn my body to face the slope, and pull myself around until I can step on a narrow terrace. There is another rock outcropping ahead of me, and the rain is falling heavily now and she has disappeared again. And I realize that her dress is not as bright because it is wet; she is soaked through with the rain, and I know that she must be leading me to shelter.

I cling to the mountainside and try to orient myself. I know that the Temple of the Moon is in a cavern halfway up the north face of Huayna Picchu. The trail to the hidden temple leads off the main path, but to the left, and I have gone to the right and I am too high—the peak is scarcely a hundred feet above me. I look back to where she disappeared, but it is difficult to focus on the boulder in the falling rain and a cloud scuds across the moon and the sliver-gray night fades to black and I move forward, hugging the slope and placing my feet with great care, safe from slipping from the friction of my body against the mountainside. It is a chamber whose entrance is hidden in a fold of granite by the edge of a terrace that no farmer could ever have tended. It is a long chamber twenty feet deep by the sulfur flare of my match. When the match burns down and I drop it to the floor, the blackness is blacker than the night that is framed by the irregular lips of this little cave.

There is no sign of the little girl. Outside the rain is falling, and the blackness of the cavern reverberates with a sound that is like a long hush.

I wipe the rain from my face and sit with my back to the rock wall.

And then I close my eyes.

There was a hut or hovel in the snow. Beside an outcrop of jagged granite that pierces the ice, there was a dwelling made of earth. I saw it from a tree, a bare spindly tree, naked in the winter. A small bundle of herbs, dried and brittle gray and brown twigs with tiny desiccated yellow blossoms, was hanging from one of the branches. The air was perfectly still because the smoke from the hut rose, from an opening in the roof, in a perfectly straight line. I could smell the dryness in the air.

To my left was a gentle white slope rising only a hundred feet or so to the fine black horizon, crisp and distinct in the clear, clean, motionless air of the place. To my right, over the granite outcrop, the mountain fell to a dark valley. I knew where the snow line ended: two hundred feet down the embankment. Behind me was the vista of snowclad peaks and green valleys gray in the night—a succession of whites and grays, peaks and valleys, as far as I could . . . feel them.

I describe these sights in terms of their orientation, but I saw them all at once. I was aware of what was around me, ahead, left, right, behind, up and down. And my senses had lost their distinction. To say that I smelled the dryness in the air, that I felt the peaks and valleys that stretched into the distance, is just a literary trick, but it is the closest I can come to describing a feeling of common sense. This phenomenon was tested inside the hut, where there were colors to listen to and textures to taste.

I will not belabor these metaphors. Just imagine that you are a sphere, like a bubble in a glass of champagne, and your surface reflects everything, because *everything* is reflected on the surface of a perfect sphere. Your experience is not specific to your spatial orientation—you experience everything that is there simultaneously. And you experience them with all of your senses so that textures, aromas, flavors, sounds, and colors, are felt, smelled, tasted, heard, and seen simultaneously.

I moved into the hut and I could smell the orange heat of a fire in an earthen oven. There was a thick candle on a wooden table, and I was drawn to it and hovered there; and the thick woven mat of many colors on the hard-packed dirt floor, and the walls covered with plants and animal and insect things drying, and the sputter of the candle flame guttering, and the liquid pearls of candle wax spilling, and the woman there—all were reflected on the perfect sphere of my awareness.

She was an old woman, a native face with a hundred lines and gray eyes and peppery gray hair parted in the middle and braided on one side, and the braid was tied off with a strip of woven ribbon. Her mouth and her hands were moving. She was talking about me; rudely, she would not look at me, although she clearly acknowledged my presence because she disapproved. Her lips were moving and her eyebrows, which were nothing more than a few scant gray hairs above her drooping eyelids, were drawn into a frown that pulled all those lines on her forehead down to the bridge of her nose. Her hands were moving too; they were busy making candles out of animal lard. Her hands and yellow fingernails were greasy with it.

All of this, every sense of it that can be described, I took in without a thought. My first thought was that I was dreaming; it was a fact that I was dreaming, I was *aware* that I was dreaming.

And then the room collapsed as if the bubble sphere that I was, hovering there by the candle, burst; and in the dream I see myself, sitting before the Pachamama Stone, and the dancers are moving in the soft rain and the orange light of the fire. I knew that somewhere I was in my body and dreaming about myself watching the dancers down there with the seedpods and the nutshells shaking. *That* is a dream. And *this?* I was back in the hut then and the woman's face was at me—so close that I could see the pores in her nose and her awful scowling face as she drew on the bone bit of a hardwood pipe and blew reeking pungent smoke over the surface of me. She seemed resigned to my being there; and although I could not *hear* her words, her lips moved and I know that she told me to follow her.

I moved beside her, near her right shoulder, which was covered with a black alpaca shawl, and she trudged through the snow—her feet crunched through the ice crust and sunk deep into the snow, and the ribboned hem of her long and heavy woven wool dress brushed along the ice and collected tiny crystals of frost. Her coca-smelling breath made warm vapor clouds that puffed out and dissipated along the sides of her face as she bent to the task of walking down the slope and climbing over rocks—until we came to an awful, jagged place of rock, below the snow line and hidden behind a crag. Over the top was a little V-shaped flat space among the rocks, and a middle-aged tree with a few dead leaves still clinging.

And there on the ground were two birds, hideous in every aspect; I sensed them completely—I am an orb that is fully aware and experiencing things with all my senses, and I am revolted and fascinated by my sense of the condors that hopped and jerked around a pulpy red mess of flesh and fur and bones and entrails in the dirt between them.

Condor, from the Quechua word, *kúntur*. *Vultur gryphus*. They were the size of dogs—one was larger than the other—all black and gray, wings half-cocked—six feet each when extended—and their heads were deformations of necks that protruded from a flounce of fluffy gray feathers, and their faces were long and wrinkled pink, ending in a snub bone-yellow beak hooked over like a curved, jaundiced toenail. Their eyes were shiny black beads. Their feathers rustled as their wings beat against each other as they danced around the dead animal and jabbed at it with a mindless violence. And although I knew that this was some perversion of a dream state—that somewhere I was asleep and dreaming about the dancers in Machu Picchu— I knew also that this was not the time to probe the experience. Something important was going to happen here.

I was taught how to capture them. The old crone closed her eyes, then opened them, and she taught me then and there, downwind of the great endangered birds, how to project myself into an animal. They were wary— some animals are less susceptible than others; and as we began to trick them with our will, they became alarmed and their heads jerked up—mine still had a morsel of raw flesh stuck comically on the side of its beak. I learned fast, learned that you can merge with their simple consciousness and inhabit their being for as long as you like.

It happened in a moment, when the beast swung its head around and I caught it through the eyes. Then I was with it and it was scared. Fight-or-flight reflex for a bird means flight, and I left the ledge with it and soared through the night in a flight of such ecstasy that I shiver to think of it. Because of the height, the sheer speed of the free-fall, wing-tucked descent, the effortless ascent, and soundless circles inscribed in the blackness above the valley, I could have flown it to death, the giddy rocket that I rode face-first through the night. I could have killed the bird, exhausted it, but I took it instead out over the ravine that plunged from the peak of the *apu* to the river below, then back to the hut in the snow where the crone waited for me, drew me back in. I left the bird hopping around on the ice-crusted snow and I hovered again by the candle, while she warmed herself by the clay oven and her lips moved and she made me know that I should go. I had not been invited, and if I came again I would need to announce myself by shaking the herb bundle that hung on the tree outside her door.

I tried to go back to my dream. I knew that I had to be dreaming again to wake up; and when I see myself sleeping in the meadow before the Pachamama Stone, I struggle to wake myself. The dancers have gone and dawn is threatening to break and I am asleep on the grass that is still wet with the night's rain and I cannot wake myself. It is only when I see myself stir and watch my eyes open that I realize that I am dreaming of myself waking in the meadow. I watch myself elbow myself up from the ground and witness myself staring at the trampled mud—the marks of the dancer's leather-shod feet in the trampled grass and mud. No, I told myself, I am still dreaming. I am stuck between sleeping and waking, stuck in this dream and I must wake from this.

I did, of course, wake from the dream; the vision of myself waking in the meadow and inspecting the traces of the dancers was the dream from which I woke. And when finally I emerged from that stuck place, I was not in the meadow at all. I was in the cavern in the side of Huayna Picchu.

I was stiff and sore. When I stood and arched my back, muscles strained and joints popped and a wave of nausea swelled in my empty stomach as I recalled the sensation of that common sense that I had experienced in the night. Curiously the memory of my disoriented awareness—my free-floating *sensation* of the old woman, her front and back and sides and smell and flavor and sound and feel—caused me to waver with a feeling like motion sickness. It was early, around 6:30 A.M., and I stepped unsteadily out onto the narrow lip of terrace and looked down before I looked up. It was a dizzying drop down a mostly granite face—the northeastern face of the mountain. I lifted my gaze from the river and the train station 2,000 feet below me, and followed with my eyes the road that winds back and forth, turns on itself seven times in a crazy zig-zag up the Machu Picchu hillside, and composed myself by leveling my gaze on the ruins.

Everything was in a haze of early morning fog and low overcast—everything except the ruins. Machu Picchu was spread out below me in its perfect stillness, and an irregular light shone down on it and highlighted places in the city with bright splashes of color. The source of this strange light was a rend in the clouds, a jagged tear that glowed golden-white against the gray ceiling, and the rays of sunlight that had punched through were defined by the morning mist and beamed down on sections of walls and half-temples and the long concourse of the main plaza. This flaw in the sky would open, I knew; with time—in an hour or so—the gash in the clouds would widen and the gloom would part and the city would warm to the day in the April Sun.

PART III

LIFE IN DEATH

10

I will show you fear in a handful of dust.

—*T. S. Eliot*

AS I SLIPPED AND SLID DOWN THE SOUTHWESTERN
slope of Huayna Picchu that morning, I stopped for a moment with my back
to the vertical hillside and wondered if I had wakened to the right reality.
It was a daunting thought and numbed me for a moment. But what could
I do? How could I take stock of my sensations and be reassured that I was
heading down the hill to the ridge that led back to the Pachamama Stone—
to all that was familiar? How could I be sure that an afternoon would follow the morning, and a night would follow the afternoon, and I would live
through them in a manner that I was accustomed to living, breathing, func-
tioning with an awareness that was familiar? But all of those sensations on
the morning after my adventure in the meadow and on the mountain—the
physical discomfort, the perceptual ambiguities—*were* familiar; I had lived
through many such mornings returned from some realm of consciousness
that had been nothing like I expected, my range of awareness redefined,
my head swimming with possibilities, my gut gripped with a strangely ecstatic anxiety at once to understand what I had lived, to validate it, and to
articulate it.

Unfortunately the man who had always been there either to support
my disbelief or to verify my interpretations was missing.

Headed for the jungle because there is nowhere else to go—I have no one to turn to but Ramón, no way to contact Antonio but to return to the jungle. I am fully aware now that I am in the middle of something I do not understand. The more I turn events over in my mind, the more I am sure that something extraordinary is brewing and the more I suspect that any analysis is premature.

Two nights ago at the Pachamama Stone, I meditated myself into an ecstatic state and found myself in the midst of a vision of native dancers in Inca-style dress engaged in a ceremony around a fire in the meadow. They threw offerings of flowers and herbs and the air was sweet with incense. The details were exquisite, I cannot recall anything so utterly vivid. It had none of the qualities that I am accustomed to in a self-induced trance state—there was nothing particularly flexible or abstract about it. It was the most clearly defined lucid dream that I have ever experienced.

I followed a little Indian girl from the circle of dancers up the steep trail on Huayna Picchu. In the dark, in the rain. I cannot separate this episode from reality, because I woke up in a small cave near the peak. I remember the hike up the mountainside and closing my eyes in the cave and then—

I was in a winter landscape that could have been Alaska, but I am sure that it was one of the snowbound peaks—Salcantay or Ausangate. I do not remember feeling altitude because I do not remember breathing in the state I was in. A comprehensive state of awareness that followed no rules. It was a common sense of things, in which all of my senses were stimulated to respond simultaneously to what was there. It did not bother me at the time—there was something dizzying about it—but later, when I recalled the sensation, it was like too much of too many rich foods and there was something nauseating about it, the richness of it all was overwhelming.

In the midst of it, though, I was disoriented only, and when I began to analyze the sensation I collapsed back into the "dream" I was having of the dancers. So I knew that somewhere I had left my body dreaming something. I could return to that dream if necessary, but I stayed for a while in this hut where an old crone—who reminded me of the old woman who sat beside me when I witnessed the death of Antonio's teacher years ago—was making candles. She was irritated or inconvenienced by my presence, but resigned to it. All this while I was an orb floating in space beside a candle on her table. She was preparing for something, but I do not know what it was. Finally she "took" me outside—I followed her out into the snow and she walked until we came upon a scene of two condors—giant Andean condors—feasting off some dead animal, maybe a rabbit. And she taught me how to project my intent into them—how to capture an animal's consciousness—and for a short while, I think I flew with one of them. She told me to "announce" myself the next time I came, and then I returned to the dream. And in the dream I was asleep. I was dreaming of myself asleep in the meadow before the Pachamama Stone and I saw myself waking up and looking at the traces the dancers had left in the mud.

There was a real sense of panic then, as I knew that I was stuck in this dream that I was dreaming and I had to wake up. When I did wake up, it was all of a sudden—the image simply snapped off when I opened my eyes in the cave in Huayna Picchu.

So I induce a trance state, an altered state that allows me to witness the dancers. Then I climb Huayna Picchu and fall asleep there. I am then in this common sense state that is to a dream what a dream is to the waking state. Is this the dream *time*? Distinct and separate from the dream *state*? I am guessing that it is. When I fell asleep in the cave, I *dreamed* about the dancers that I had left in the meadow, and then *left* that dream and entered this dream time, where the old woman taught me things and I was nothing but a free-floating ball of consciousness with some sort of omniscient sensory perception. When I left the dream time, I was back in the dream state, dreaming about the dancers, and later dreaming of myself waking in the meadow—but I was still asleep in the cave all the while.

Is this what I came to Peru to experience?

That was how I summarized it all, two days later, on a plane bound for Pucallpa.

The morning after my night on Huayna Picchu, after retrieving my backpack from my nook in the ruins, I had taken coffee and a pastry with one of the watchmen whom I had known for years. We had bumped into each other near the entrance to the ruins; he was coming in and I was going out, and I know that he was alarmed at my condition. He was used to seeing me leading a group of well-fed and mostly fit Americans and Europeans fresh from Cuzco, and now there I was, solo, a pack on my back and looking like hell: four days on the trail, four days' growth of beard, four days of sunburn in spite of my hat, all of it rained on in the night. The way down the mountain had all but destroyed my trousers, and my boots were caked with mud. He looked me up and down after a hearty greeting, and asked me how long I had been here.

"Only last night," I said, and watched his eyes move past me into the ruins and up, under raised eyebrows, to the presiding peak of Huayna Picchu. There was something respectful in his uplifted gaze and then, as though addressing both the mountain and me:

"It went well?"

I nodded. *"Como siempre,"* I said. As always.

He led me back to his hut. We drank coffee and ate bread and he showed me his cache of the most recent artifacts that he had uncovered on the edge of the digs that were always half-started and underfunded around the ruins.

It was too early for the minibus that hauls people up and down the zig-zag road between the train station and the ruins, and I did not feel like waiting. So I walked down the winding dirt road and caught the return leg of the first arriving round-trip train from Cuzco.

I spent a day in Cuzco. I had left a change of clean clothes at the hotel, and the owner of the Café Garcilaso across the street took in my laundry. I showered and ate and slept for most of the day.

Twenty-four hours later I was flying north to Pucallpa. I had made up my mind on the train, and I never took the time to change it. I set off half-cocked for the jungle with the notion that Ramón could help me find Antonio. Although the compassionate old Quechua professor and the taciturn *ayahuascero* had never met in the flesh, they had been aware of each other even before I had come on the scene fifteen years ago. When I was looking for an *ayahuascero* to demonstrate the effects and use of the "vine of the dead," Antonio had given me directions for finding Ramón in his Amazon hideaway, and I knew that they shared a respect for each other for which I had become a conduit; they had their prodigious skills and me in common.

I would not look to Ramón for counseling; the incident in Machu Picchu was more in Antonio's domain.

Antonio had been the first to describe to me the Medicine Wheel, the journey of the Four Winds. On that occasion, fifteen years ago, he said that few complete the journey, that there are few shamans of the North— few true persons of knowledge. Many who tread this path, he said, stop along the way and are content to be healers and medicine people; they become masters of the South or the West, but not master shamans. Ramón was a healer and master of the West, where fear and death are called upon, formulated, and exorcised from the psyche. And although he believed that to exorcise fear one must exorcise violence and live compassionately, he was the most feared man of the region. He was a wizard of the *ayahuasca*. He was a cantankerous old man who dwelled in the primeval Eden of the Amazon, cultivating his plants and fungi and brewing his medicines and serving as healer to the tribes who had lived in this dark garden of the world for centuries. But he was not a master shaman, a "person of knowledge"; that distinction, I had learned, was Antonio's. But in seeking Antonio Morales, don Ramón Silva was my only ally.

So I flew to the Pucallpa airstrip, waited two long hours for the bus, and headed down the heat-fractured and pockmarked strip of pavement called the Trans Amazon Highway. After a bone-jarring hour and a half, I asked the driver to let me off at kilometer 64—a once whitewashed signpost with faded numbers buried in the dust-caked foliage at the side of the highway.

The bus engine revved and gears ground and it made a sound like a death rattle and shuddered off down the road, leaving me in a cloud of poisonous diesel fumes that hung like excrement, motionless in the heat.

I pushed my way through the swelter and crossed the road and penetrated the tangle and followed the path that I knew was there. It is a path that you only recognize if you are on it, so thick is the overgrowth. The jungle floor was soft and springy. Overhead the canopy of crisscrossed vines and fanlike branches and mammoth leaves cut the sunlight into chunks that dappled the path like spots on a leopard. There were dripping orchids and fuzzy creepers and elephant-ear palms and ferns that fringed the trail, and I walked for thirty minutes, stopping only once to close my eyes and listen to the whir and click and hum of the jungle—the thousands of rhythms that play together and in counterpoint to produce the steady drone of this place—and to remember that my associations with this botanical garden paradise were inseparable from this staccato chorus of living things.

Ramón's three-room, thatch-roofed home sits in a clearing beside a lagoon that is really a backwater of a tributary of the great river whose source is the Andes and whose effluence is the Atlantic. It used to be a two-room, L-shaped hut, but he had recently added a sort of veranda: on stilts, an open-air platform with half-walls of woven palm fronds like wainscoting that half enclosed the perimeter around the bamboo floor. There were fewer chickens than I remembered, and no sign of the pigs and goats that normally wandered the enclave at the ends of long tethers. Only two ducks swam in the lagoon—there were usually more—and they pecked at the watery fringe of algae-covered roots and sagging leaves and waterlogged branches on the opposite bank.

This was a place that I had mythologized, sanctified in my imagination for all of the magical things that had happened there. I had first seen the Sachamama, the serpent spirit of the South, a twenty-foot jungle boa, leave me and slither across the surface of this lagoon and disappear in a black gap in the far phosphorescent shore. I had stood here on the sandy edge of this lagoon, stood entranced in the night by my own reflection—my rippled face stared brightly back at me from its dark glassy surface—and then dipped my hand and pinched the reflection and lifted it, like the skin that forms on the surface of a cup of cocoa; I had lifted my own limp, sodden reflection from the surface of this lagoon and stared at it twisting into a liquid stringiness and dripping onto the sand.

And Antonio, upon hearing my description of the lagoon and my experiences there, had used this place as a metaphor although he had never seen it, not with his own two eyes. In his mind's eye this lagoon became a poetic expression of the human psyche. The surface that you see, he had said to me, is dependent upon what lies below. The unseen depths support the surface; but looking at the surface from the shore, you can only guess at what lies below. It could be very deep; there could be plants waiting to entangle, dangerous currents, *pirañas*, even. Fear keeps you from penetrating its depths. But if you change your perspective on the water, see where the Sun shines on the surface, and look at it from above—where the eagle flies—you might see what lies below. Once you have acquired such vision, you will know the lagoon and may swim with impunity.

This was how he had once described the process of perceiving the unconscious; it was a matter of shifting one's perspective and looking at something from an unaccustomed dimension. I had thought at the time that his metaphor was charming but somewhat prosaic; it was, after all, nothing more than comparing the human mind to a body of water, and that had been done before: conscious mind and unconscious mind, the surface of the sea and its unseen depths. But then I had not known Antonio for very long.

Now I stared at the ducks on the opposite shore of the lagoon, the reflection of the banana and elephant-ear palms and ferns and vine-tangled tree trunks—the wall of jungle that formed an enclave around its banks and were mirrored on its surface. I noticed where the Sun glistened in playful white sparkles of light on its green waters. I listened to the cicada hiss, the high-pitched cacophony of the birds and the insects, the whir and hiss and chatter and hum that bounced off its surface and filled the clearing with music. And I remembered Antonio's response to my charge.

"I did not compare the mind to a pond," he had said. "I compared it to that lagoon that frightened you. A lagoon is part of a stream. It is a place where the shore widens and the center deepens and the water slows, but the water is, nevertheless, constantly flowing through it. I can even travel upstream, nearer the source, and affect the lagoon in any number of ways by affecting its source. I can place an object in the stream, and eventually, if nothing interferes along the way, it will reach the lagoon, and if it stays there long enough, it might sink in. I can place my hand in the water and cause a ripple in the stream that will eventually reach the lagoon and reverberate through it. It might even upend the canoe you are sitting in, or save you by washing you ashore." And so he had spun out his metaphor like a faithful poet, creating for me a model of human consciousness as part of a greater consciousness that flows through it and informs it.

Finally, years later, I had plumbed its depths. One night when I watched the jungle liquefy and run in colorful rivulets into the lagoon, I followed them to its bottom and there I experienced my own death.

Thus had this place become sanctified in my imagination; this is how it became sacred to me—my psyche had achieved a harmony with this place and I had engaged directly with its terrain.

So I stood there in the clearing and failed to hear Ramón's approach. My memories had brought me back to my immediate purpose, which was finding Antonio. I wanted so to see him, to relate to him my adventure in Machu Picchu, to know that in some way my solo return was a response to his invitation. If Ramón was surprised or pleased to see me, his face did not show it. But he gripped my arm and led me to the close sandy bank of the lagoon where the *yagé,* the noxious smelling soup of *ayahuasca* vine married with the flavors and properties of half a dozen plant parts, boiled in an oilcan hanging from a brazier above a sunken fire-pit.

There is a tree that had grown there—or perhaps the jungle and the lagoon and the clearing had formed around it, for it is was a thousand years old when it died. Its gnarled face and exposed roots preside over the clearing like a grotesque beast that set its tentacles down into the Earth and crouches here still, waiting for something to happen. It is a *chihuahuaco* tree, a "grandfather tree," and its trunk is hollow. I have meditated within that space countless times; then it is like an enormous neuron with dendrites above and below, reaching up into the heavens and down into the Earth, branches that touch the ineffable above and roots buried in the very ground of meaning—even in wooden lifelessness, it is a place of great potency; like the Cathedral at Chartres, it has a form that inspires introspection and prayer. Now there was an empty oilcan beside it, and inside the hollow was a wooden bowl brimming with *yagé,* left there during the three nights of the full moon. My arrival was opportune. We would drink the *yagé* tonight, he said, and see what sort of death I was incubating inside of me. It had been too long, he said, since I last visited the landscape of my fears.

Waiting for the night.

Listening to the white noise of the jungle, watching the Sun set over the treetops, the shadows grow, reaching toward me across the clearing and across the surface of the lagoon.

Abiding a ritual in the nighttime.

Ramón responded to my anxiety to find Antonio with a shrug and a nod. He has had no contact with him, and respects my need to know, and he will work toward that end in this evening's work. He made me aware that the fear of coming back empty-handed—engaging in the work of the *ayahuasca* for such a specific end and failing to achieve it—was a fear that I should shed before the Sun sets, and I've given it a lot of thought. It is a challenge specific to those who have become skilled in moving through the terrain of the West that they do not fool themselves into forcing the outcome—if you carry with you an agenda, you are likely to have that agenda tested; and you cannot hold anything so dear that you are unwilling to relinquish it.

You can only *have* something that you are capable of *not* having—that is the essence of this prosaic irony. Once again, intent is the issue. Impeccability is the prerequisite.

He did comment, while looking me over in that half-distracted glazed-eyed way of his, that I had begun a new journey. That I have gone further than Augustin, if not deeper. Augustin has evidently mastered the *ayahuasca,* and he will work in this realm for the rest of his life. So I suppose that Ramón is pleased that I have elected to continue to work beyond the West, though I have never really thought about my work in those terms. We are expecting Augustin this evening.

And Ramón had expected me; he knew that I was coming, as he always has. This time he told me that a condor had preceded me by six hours—he had seen it this morning circling the clearing, and there was no carrion to feed on. He asked when I had acquired this new power animal, this new manifestation of myself in nature. It acted confused, he said (leave it to him to be able to tell the difference), and he assumed that it was new to me and I to it. I told him about my journey to Machu Picchu, and he nodded as if that explained it all. He grinned, actually, and said I was becoming more stealthy—I used to announce my arrival whole days ahead of time.

Talked about *The Four Winds*, and he was clearly pleased that our past together had been given the form of a story.

The Sendero are here—in the general vicinity. The revolutionaries have split into two factions and have allied themselves with the coca growers who have been stripping and burning huge tracts of jungle for the last five or six years. They have come to him for medical problems and healing, and have stolen some of his chickens and pigs. Ramón will, I'm sure, seek to mete out justice to the thieves in some metaphysical way that I shudder to think of. As long as they grow sick, he will heal them; but I know he is a man of Nature before he is a man of peace. Their violence to the jungle and to others is deeply disturbing to him, and he is thinking that he will move if they do not.

The telepathic influence of *ayahuasca* is well documented; the effect is so marked that certain of the organic chemical compounds that form in the *yagé* have been nicknamed "telepathine." Often I have experienced flights of remarkable distance and visions of breathtaking clarity when engaged in ritual with Ramón. Evidently Augustin was bringing with him a sample of *yagé* that he had found to be mild and remarkably "clear." They would have a *toma*—an *ayahuasca* ceremony—but I would take only a drop, a taste on the tip of tongue, participate in the *toma* symbolically. We decided that the best way for me to work was independent of the medicine. The environment and the intent would serve me best. Ramón was more confident of my skills than I was, but we both agreed that an unfamiliar preparation of *yagé* might serve to distract me, seduce me with opportunities.

Augustin was an old friend, a native of Pucallpa and a fellow student of don Ramón Silva's. He is in his late fifties, although he sometimes looks eighty and has the charm of a cheerful adolescent; he is vigorously masculine, yet he has an air of innocent androgyny. His kindness and charity have become bywords in Pucallpa, where he practices his shamanic art with a skill and precision that has made him the most important and respected healer of the town.

He came up from behind me. I was sitting on the sand, facing the lagoon. I heard him coming and sensed his stealthy footsteps in the sand but I showed no sign. I let him surprise me, cover my eyes with his stiff, claw-like hands—an accident had severed tendons in his forearms and wrists, and the fleshy part of his palms and his hands are permanently deformed—and ask why I had called this primitive medical convention in the jungle.

"I am looking for Antonio," I said, "and any excuse to come here is a good excuse."

"Ramón told me you would be here," he said. "We spoke to each other on the night of the full moon. I think you were in Machu Picchu."

The ritual began late in the night when the moon was high and the cadence of the chorus of the jungle, its audible heartbeat, had quickened to an *allegro,* because the jungle sleeps in the heat of the day and awakens at dusk.

It began with an invocation to the Four Winds and the spirits of the jungle. We sat on mats of woven palm fronds on the bamboo floor of Ramón's veranda. We smoked heartily from Augustin's carved hardwood pipe the dense and chokingly rich tobacco that Ramón had grown and cured there in the jungle. And they drank the *yagé* that Augustin had brought from the jungle near Iquitos, three hundred miles north-north-west. For me there was a drop, a token taste. Ramón dipped the wooden stem of the pipe into the bowl and carried one pendant drop to the tip of my tongue.

An hour later I left them. I was inspired to wander to a place in the jungle where I had meditated before. I left them in a state of harmony; Augustin, the nubile old man and former student, played a tune on a curved hardwood bow—a one-stringed harp held to his mouth, which moved to form the syllables of the notes that his crooked finger plucked on the single string.

I have held misery in my arms. When I was very young, I met a woman and we were lovers. She was love itself; and by this I mean that she lived in her heart, and her heart was an open house where any invited could stay for free. I filled this house with my presence, although its design displeased me, and I feigned comfort—for it was, at least, a shelter.

I remember holding her close when we knew that it was over. I remember how it felt to embrace her grief, how her sobs, her breathless agony, shook me. I had denied her gift of love. I had taken as much of it as I could hold before my conscience forced me to stop taking.

I move with a lithesomeness that I am used to in this place, shadowlike through a place of shadows. Truly the drop of *yagé* has produced no appreciable effect, and this is ideal for the use to which I will put myself as soon as I find my ruin. The place that I am looking for, moving toward, surely, is a clearing a hundred feet into the jungle. A structure, some sort of temple, is embedded there, unvisited by any but Ramón, perhaps, and known only to the occasional Shipibo or Campas Indian who might wander from the banks of the river. It is a charming relic dressed in jungle finery; orchids cling to wedges of soil between its stones, and vines and creeping plants hang like gaudy necklaces across its walls. It sits like the archetypal picture of mystery from a nineteenth-century explorer's lithograph, in a tiny clearing east of Ramón's complex. I have had the finest of experiences there; it is where I first felt the strange schizophrenia of inhabiting another consciousness when I stalked myself, sitting in meditation in the moonlight in the center of the clearing, and opened my eyes to see the cat, the full-grown black and vaguely spotted jaguar that I had been, standing, panting, three feet away.

Now I sought this place for its solitude. Washed in the light of the near-full moon, it would be the ideal place to unleash my mind and access Antonio's.

But I missed it. In the dark density of the jungle, I missed the path that was at best only a suggestion of a trail, and I found myself walking much farther than I had intended. I doubled back and zig-zagged my way through the foliage, decided I had passed it again, that there were trees and flora that were familiar over . . . there, so I pushed on, only to lose myself more thoroughly.

I stop and laugh at the idiocy of it all. I cough out my anger. I am not here to lose myself like a child awkwardly, blindly stumbling through this place, when I have such a purpose as this evening's. I did not come to Peru to get myself lost. So I abandon the effort and decide to head for the river. Its banks will serve me as well.

But there is a stench in the air, like rotten fruit, muskier than the lush pungency that hangs always in the liquid heat of the Amazon. I keep my eyes to the ground, stepping carefully to avoid catching my ankles in the crisscross of creepers and vines that run across the jungle floor like swollen veins and arteries. A confusion of leaves and branches blocks my way, and I brush them aside and feel something slimy on my fingers and palm. I look carefully, and the leaves are shiny with a mucousy film that I wipe on my pant leg.

The farther I go, the deeper the decay. All things are gray in the night, for the colors of life are made by the Sun that gives life. But I can see the life that inhabits the jungle—I am used to seeing the subtle light that radiates from living things in this place, in this state of consciousness, and the light is failing, not because of me—I am perceiving clearly, I know—but the life is fleeing, the plants are fading, and their flesh is withering with every step I take.

Something is terribly wrong. I stop in the empty silence and terrible stillness of a dead world. I shiver involuntarily; a spasm grips my body and moves through it like an electrical charge because the melody, the dynamic, the melodynamic of the Amazon has ceased without crescendo and the sound is the sound that they say is in space, the sound of me, the blood shushing between thudding heartbeats. The insects and birds have hushed in midphrase, and this is not the sound of suspended expectation, the breathless quiet that precedes the smell of a white man in the garden—it is the silence of a vacuum, an airless place—that is it—a place where there is no air to carry sound, and that is why the only sound is my own carried to my ears because it vibrates through my body that conducts the sound to my ears, but that is all. My neck cracks as I move it left to look at the silence, and all that I see is lifelessness. I have reached the place where the plants are hollow husks through which nothing moves—to my right a banana palm, juiceless, its skin translucent because everything that flowed and filled the cell walls and gave it shape has ceased to flow and dried away and there is nothing left but dead fibers in the unmoving air—an orchid there near the base of the tree ruined and gone after its flesh swelled and burst and the life ran out of it—other things blackened as though poisoned from within. And that is all there is. It is black and gray and sickly white, a landscape abandoned by life, and I gasp and choke on my inhalation. There in the air is the smell of the death, the reek of the emptiness, the ghost of the putrification that had hung here in the dust when everything died.

It is in the soil. I fall to my knees and hear the sound of them crackle the leaves and mulch dry as dust, so that I know for a certainty that I *can* hear—that there is lack of sound because nothing moves here anymore—and I plunge my hands into the stale soil and my fingers dig desperately down, claw frantically through layers of arid soil to where it is spoiled and rank with all the plasma turned poisonous and reclaimed back into the Earth, withdrawn from the bodies that it killed, recalled through every cell and fiber and vein until the jungle is a graveyard of sapless corpses, flimsy shells of once living things, and I draw my hands, sticky with the stuff, up to me and grunt my despair and the breath from my lungs exsiccates the very dankness from it and I feel it tremble so subtly as the moisture leaves it, retreats from the surface of the sodden mulch in my hands.

Understand, as I understood, that it was me that the poisoned moisture retreated from, it was the air that I exhaled and the sweat that I spilled, and the tears, and the very smell of me, the essence of me, even the very intent that preceded my movement through the jungle poisoned it, toxicated it, turned the mineral and nutrient-bearing waters that fed it into noxious stuff that the Earth drew back into herself that it might not evaporate in the morning and rise to the clouds and rain down on the rest of the Earth. She took the poison that I spread into herself. I understand in that instant that it is I who am responsible, that she has begun to incorporate into her own flesh the foulness that I excrete so that the disease that I cause will not spread. But how can she stay ahead of me? She will only save herself if I stop. And I scream it out into the perfect stillness of that night.

And that is why I say that I have held misery in my arms and the misery of the lover that I misled was nothing to the misery of the Earth that trembled at my touch. Human suffering knows nothing, can speak to nothing compared to what I felt quaking there below the matted floor of the ruined jungle.

Yes, it was all perceived in a realm of consciousness where death dwells and the very spirit of fear constitutes itself. For although I am not reacting to the token taste of the *ayahuasca,* I know the realm. I have seen the dreadful manifestations of this domain invade my awareness by invitation because, in my work of the West, dutifully I had invited fear and welcomed death to come and claim me. And I have seen the jungle liquefy and run in phosphorescent rivulets into Ramón's lagoon, and I have sunk to its bottom and watched myself die on the desert sand beneath the surface and lost all sensation and felt the rigor and the mortis that followed; I had moved free from my own corpse and followed a jaguar black as a shadow toward the light that one hears so much about from all those who have survived near-death; and I had joined that light for an instant, when all that I knew echoed in the brightness and all that I had seen reflected every other sight infinitely and I had died and maintained my consciousness through death. And I have become a "spirit warrior" with no enemies in this lifetime or the next. I walked in the snow without leaving tracks because I no longer feared death, for death cannot claim one who has already died, lived the experience of death, learned to know it for what it really is. Oh, and I have seen and felt many other things of extraordinary beauty in subsequent experiences with the *ayahuasca,* all to the tune of Ramón's or Augustin's songs and the reverbs of their one-string harps and the constant white-noise of the jungle chorus. But I had been in meditation then, motionless in my body, moving only through the domain of the experience. And the death had always been mine. But this was not my death I was living—although, very soon now, it would be.

In this moment I know that the Earth is dying, and I and those who will soon crash through this charnel with killing me on their minds are her killers. I am a child of hers, and my brothers and sister are legion. We each of us have done this now, I know, and the agony of this spoiled dirt in my hands runs to the core of the planet that bore us into life.

Is there anything conceivable that revolts the mind like the evidence of disease spread by a son to his mother—a venereal disease passed from child to parent by . . . molestation? The evidence is unavoidable in my hands now; I attest to it. And my tears fall on it and crystallize like the hard chemical things that they are.

And I know that I cannot live with the knowledge; every unwholesome cell of my body screams with self-hate. And inflicted with this fatal emotion, I rise in the silence and move forward with awkward purposelessness, until the sounds of my killers cause me to run with one last contradictory impulse to survive after all.

Sendero, undoubtedly. Jungle guerrillas, fanatical, ignorant of their intent, addled by violence, blind with self-interest, camouflaged in social reform, like any revolutionaries, hypocritical and drunk with the freedom of maniacal extremes. My assassins.

A round of automatic-weapon fire burps in the stillness behind me, and it would have silenced the jungle for a heartbeat if it had been alive to hear it. I am; and their shouts and laughter reach out and tickle the back of my neck.

And I fall face first through a dying fern. I lift my face away from a spore-covered frond, and there are the veins that run along every leaflet, desiccated, shriveling and hardening beneath my gaze, the vascular system failed, poisoned by the rank stuff that the soil is even now extracting. It will whither and rot like everything else I touch with my own two eyes, or *they* touch, my pursuers thrashing through the silenced garden with raging single-mindlessness.

I roll off the plant, out from the dying mess of overlapping rottenness, and push myself up from the stench of the pulp that my hands sink into up to the wrists. I am bleeding now; even I can smell it, the metallic tang of my own blood over the smell of death that is everywhere, and I know that if there are any creatures left alive in the jungle, they can smell it too; and they will rejoice that an end to me will be an end to their suffering, because their suffering and all this death is happening in my heart.

The thought explodes white-hot like a supernova, leaving short-lived brilliant insight burning there before me. It *is* my death that I am smelling—there is a gash in my leg, across my thigh, and the threads of torn trouser fabric have worked their way into the wound and that pant leg is sodden now, the blood is black in the night—but the smell is also the sensing of the death coming fast on my heels now; it will take me from behind and paralyze me first.

I run and stumble from the voices and the thrashing sounds that follow me. There is no reasoning with them. I have violated the space that they have inhabited with their lawlessness, and no words can save me; if a man dies in the jungle, he makes no sound, for there is no one to hear him die. I am a North American with eyes who has strayed into territory claimed by ruthlessness for one brief instant. How Ramón and Augustin could have let me go, knowing who had infested this place does not occur to me then, and later only briefly.

Now all is still a soundless and rotted-out garden landscape. Only my footfalls and theirs reach my ears, sensitive in the absence of all other sound—until I fall down a sudden dip in the decomposing ground, slide on my ass down a rancid embankment, and lie still, staring up at the shard of night sky visible between the interlocking leafless branches of dead trees.

I close my eyes and a last thought is definitive. It is a final revelation, a last-minute truth captured in a frozen moment of perfect stillness: The child must die for the mother to live. The Earth will abide. When all my efforts should have been focused on my survival, I thought instead that the death that we avoid, even we who have met it before, is the very solution to the disease that we have spread through the Earth. I know suddenly that the death of our species—the extinction of humanity—is ecologically inevitable. The Earth will reject her children.

The Earth will shed the life that clings to her, like a serpent sheds its skin. And trees will fall in the forest. And no one will hear them.

And the silence that attends my vision is shredded by the scream of a jungle cat. It is a sound that splits the air: On one side of it is all of Nature corrupted dead and dying, and on the other is life itself. Again the animal screams, an endless caterwauling shriek, and there is another burst of gunfire, another strident howl. It is behind me and the air quivers with its echo.

I am frozen in anticipation. An academic sort of curiosity has overtaken me, and I listen for the next sound, the next movement, the resolution of a drama that I cannot see, happening in the tangle of dead things behind me.

And the next thing I hear is the whisper of the insects. A bird, maybe a macaw, clucks out a rapid-fire warning cry, and the cicadas fill in their sibilant song and the jungle is breathing again. The next thing I see is a face that to this day quickens my heart.

Thinking of it now, I can only sigh, press the heels of my hands into my eyes, and relish the utter unbelievability of it. Try as I have to dispel what happened next from the story of my experiences, I can do nothing but faithfully tell that the young man who stood there, wide-eyed and glistening with sweat, straight black hair matted to his forehead in long, narrow triangles across his brow, was my friend from the Andes. The single-minded student who had left Machu Picchu for Vilcabamba stood there beside a living *chihuahuaco* tree. His face was drawn with urgency and he motioned for me to follow him.

He was stripped to the waist, his pants held up by a colorful woven ribbon of knotted cloth, his back was streaming with sweat as he ran a jogging course through the jungle.

I do not know how long we ran this way.

I am dizzy with fatigue and confusion. The chain reaction of colliding realities fogs my brain and I have lost blood; a fever simmers under my skin. I call to him, *Wait,* but he never falters ahead of me. He stops to brush away leaves that choke our path. *Stop,* but he shakes his head from side to side and moves on.

I cannot hear anything behind me now but the sounds of the jungle that drown out the sounds of my friend, who clears the path before me.

We emerged from the jungle onto a lip of mud and sand. There were people there, Campas Indians, dark-skinned and short-statured, three men and some canoes. The men wore white pants decorated with light geometric designs. They had uniform bowl-shaped haircuts, and one carried a long bow and a bundle of arrows tied with a leather thong. The others had shotguns. I remember the tableau of these men turning with sudden alarm as I stumbled out from the break and onto the sand. They drew back, their faces wide open in alarm; they staggered back away from us and into the shallow river up to their knees.

My young friend was no longer at my side. I remember the sound of something moving fast away, back into the jungle.

The Indians took me to Ramón's. Several miles up river, they took me in one of the dugout canoes. They use short-handled, round paddles; and since they live on the river, they are remarkably skilled at navigating it both upstream and down.

It was early morning; the Sun was up by the time we rounded a familiar bend. The jungle settled with the day as it always does; the tempo shifted imperceptibly to an *adagio* at the break of dawn, and the garden was humming to a meditative rhythm as the Sun warmed the air and coaxed the moisture from the leaves. I lay in the boat, shoulders pressed against the rough-hewn sides of its narrow hull. I had fallen asleep at one point, so I had little sense of how long of a trip we had made by the time we ran aground on the sandbank just beyond the edge of Ramón's clearing.

I thanked them, and asked them to follow me to Ramón's for food and drink. Ramón knew them by name, and they spoke together in the native tongue while we cleaned the wound in my thigh and Augustin prepared a poultice that would heal the wound in less than a week.

The Indians told Ramón that I had appeared from out of the jungle near their village and frightened them.

And I was not alone.

They said that when I emerged from the tree line there was a shadow with the eyes of a jaguar beside me. A very old and very black cat, they said, that walked with me out of the jungle. It had turned and fled back into the brush.

They had never seen a man who walked with such a cat.

There are two kinds of travelers: those who carry maps, and those who do not. When I was young I was one of these latter sort. I was spontaneously reckless. I moved arbitrarily through life, packing nothing but a notion that the "new" science called psychology was actually humanity's oldest study and that, somehow, I would learn how to marry the old with the new. I was fond of pointing out to critics of my impulsiveness that to know where you are going and how to get there is to follow in some other's footsteps, that those who traveled without maps are those who made the maps. My arrogance knew no bounds, but was, at least, passionate. And as a result of that attitude, I had discovered for myself that the only difference between the modern and the traditional approach to the human psyche is that the former is a study and the latter is an experience. Western psychology is a discipline of observation and deduction, and traditional or primitive psychology is a discipline of exploration.

Now, nearly forty years old, I lay on a palm mat on the sand by the lagoon and stared up into the feverish blue Amazon sky and wondered what had become of my principles, my standard of travel. For I knew again what I had learned long ago: that the making of a journey is, in itself, the goal that we seek. How, I asked myself, could I have questioned my reasons for returning to Peru? It was clear that I came here to kick off a quest, to reengage with the journey of the Four Winds. And evidently I was experiencing the shaman's odyssey on a new and heightened level.

I had engaged in two specific rituals and, without any help from catalytic medicines, had moved within profound domains of heightened consciousness with a keenness of perception that was sublime. The homeopathic dose of *ayahuasca* was incapable of producing anything but a bitter taste in my mouth, and that my experience in the jungle was the result of a sort of placebo effect was out of the question. I had gone to the meadow in Machu Picchu to meditate, and was transported in my body to Huayna Picchu and out of my body to another realm. I had wandered through the jungle, seeking a place from which to send my mind in search of Antonio, and found myself walking in harm's way, lost in a vision of ecological tragedy, unnatural disaster, a miscarriage of Nature. I had learned something new about fear by witnessing the death of Mother Earth and very nearly inviting my own death to end the suffering.

And my young friend? The earnest Indian of my children's generation? His presence, like everything else, was unexplained, too fantastical even to ponder. And the Indians had seen a jaguar.

In the space of a week I had learned lessons, served experiences, that would change me forever. Who can perceive with multisensory perception and not be less prejudiced by the perceptions of the individual senses? Who can witness humanity's matricide-in-progress and not be responsible for stopping it, reporting it?

True, I had failed to find Antonio. But I realized as I lay there trying to penetrate beyond the blue atmosphere above me, that finding Antonio was not what being here was about.

I had, of course, found him already, but I was then still too pragmatic to realize it.

11

We only part to meet again.
Change, as ye list, ye winds; my heart shall be
The faithful compass that still points to thee.

—*John Gay*

WHEN I SAW ANTONIO HE WAS SITTING AT AN oilcloth-covered table by the open door of the café on Calle Garcilaso—across the street from my hotel, the place where I always ate breakfast, where I had bought my *quinoa* pancakes, where I had my clothes laundered.

After two days of rest with Ramón, during which we debated the wisdom of his moving to Iquitos and away from the infestation of jungle terrorists, I had returned to Cuzco. I was intent on flying back to the States, where a new life was awaiting my return.

I had met my future wife earlier that year. She had been a medical doctor in her second year of residency in internal medicine at the finest of East Coast hospitals when she joined a group I was leading to Peru. We met, provoked each other's love, and decided to spend an eternity together. She would move to the West Coast, take a year off, and apply to Stanford, where she would complete her residency—that was the goal that we would achieve; now she was busy wrapping up her East Coast affairs and preparing to move, and I was riding in a taxi from the airport to my hotel in Cuzco. My leg was bandaged with a reeking poultice—even the driver was offended—and mosquito bites that I had no memory of feeling were making my skin crawl. I was sunburned, unshaved, and altogether overwhelmed by my adventures.

There was nothing left for me but to return to San Francisco and sort through my experiences and concentrate on building a new life with my new partner. I was anticipating my departure when I stepped gingerly out of the cab, paid the driver, and caught the gleaming Rasputin eyes that smiled at me from just within the café.

Another vision? I squinted against the sunlight that bounced up from the polished cobblestones, and peered into the relative darkness of the place. He pushed himself back from the table and stood, and there was no doubt that he was Professor Antonio Morales.

Behind me, from the open door of the hotel across the street, I could hear Angelina the *lanera*, calling my name, but I paid no attention.

Antonio smiled back at me and spread his arms. His hands were held palm up as though to catch raindrops, and I went to him and he brought both hands together to cover one of mine. It was a tender meeting, with that touch of formality that had always distinguished him.

"So you are here, after all," he said. He stepped to one side and pulled out one of the painted chairs for me to join him.

"Me?" I laughed. "Those are my words, *profesor* Morales. I have been looking for you."

He said: "I understand." And then the owner of the café was tableside, asking for our order, and I noticed that the tacked-on, plasticized checkered tablecloth was bare except for a sugar bowl and a plastic cup that held a cone of paper napkins. Antonio had been waiting there.

We ordered coffee. "How long have you been here?" I asked.

"Only half an hour. I came to the hotel because I understood that you were here."

"You understood it?"

"Yes." He looked at me with an expression that I will swear was feigned innocence. "You have been in the jungle?"

"I have."

He smiled and held my eyes with his as our coffee arrived. He was older, of course, four years older than when I saw him last, and the age showed around his eyes and mouth. His hair was a shade lighter—silver and white—brushed back neatly from his dark brow. All the lines and creases on his face were weathered, worn permanently into his countenance. His nose seemed longer, sharper than I remembered, and he had grown a little moustache, the sort of pencil moustache made popular by Ronald Coleman in the early 1930s. His clothes were still outdated; I am sure that I recognized the baggy gray tropical wool suit with wide lapels and bulging pockets. His hat—a faded brown fedora—lay on its crown under his chair. And there was a stick—a knobby length of wood too short for a walking stick, and worn so smooth that I wanted to touch its patina. His hands were wrinkled and the joints slightly swollen with arthritis. I looked at his brown and bony wrist and the slightly soiled white shirt cuff that protruded an inch from his gray jacket sleeve. I watched his hand as he lifted a spoonful of coarse sugar from the bowl and carefully, steadily, lowered the spoon onto the surface of the coffee as was his habit. We both watched the brown liquid turn the color of molasses as the coffee seeped into the sugar from the edge of the spoon and the little mound was saturated crystal by crystal.

He had been in the country, he said. He had become fascinated with gardening, with cultivating rare and relatively unknown herbs and other aromatic plants. He did not walk much—by which he meant that his former wanderings as his alter ego, don Jicaram, had been limited by his advanced age.

I told him about the recently completed book of our adventures together and he listened closely. I mentioned my continuing work with groups and talked for a while about my future wife. And I told him about my dreams, the ones that forecast my expedition through the Andes. "There was a letter in the dream," I said. "I saw it there in my backpack. I don't know who it was from or what it said, but I sensed that it was an invitation . . ."

He was nodding.

". . . from you."

"It is a wonderful dream," he said.

I waited for more, but he tipped the spoon and the rich, sparkling sugar syrup slid into the coffee. Then he asked: "Is that why you came back alone to Peru?" He set aside the spoon. "Were you following a dream?"

So I told him about the night in Canyon de Chelly when I attempted to tell a story that would tell itself, the first story ever told. I told him about my meeting with the old Hopi and his assertion that I was going to Peru. I told him about the old man's reaction to the little gold owl and his token gift of a sprig of sage—for "protection." Antonio smiled at this and used a napkin to wipe away the puddle of coffee under his spoon.

"Do you have it with you?"

"The sage?"

"The owl."

I reached into my right hand trouser pocket and produced the little gold icon. He stared at it, expressionless. I set it on the tablecloth. He touched it with his forefinger. "You have used this?"

The owl: a gift from Antonio's *mesa*, from his simple collection of power objects and fetishes. Night vision and the wisdom of the darkness, the power of lost and ancient knowledge. Huayna Picchu after dark. The old shamaness. The visions of the jungle in the dead of night. Strange that it had never occurred to me to use the little owl as a focal point of my meditations, although I had carried it with me for so long that it had become a part of my effects. But it had become less significant to me as a tool; it was a relic of the past, a symbol of our friendship.

"Yes," I said, for who am I to claim that its power had not manifested itself in the course of the last week?

"And the sage?"

"No," I admitted. "I left that medicine bag at home. I forgot it."

"That is a shame," he said. "You look like you could have used it in the jungle."

"I want to talk to you about that," I said. "Something happened there, and something happened in Huayna Picchu. I would like your opinion."

"It is yours, for all that it is worth," he replied; then he did something that surprised me. For all his tenderness and affection, there was a formality to his demeanor that forbade even the subtlest physical demonstration of his feelings. That is why it surprised me when he reached out and covered my hand with his. And although he was unaccustomed to such a gesture, there was nothing awkward in the moment.

"I am glad that you have come," he said. "I am preparing for a journey, an excursion, that I think you will enjoy."

In that moment I would have accompanied him the way Dante went with Virgil to hell and back, so strong was my affection for the old man. But he had something else in mind, although no less dramatic.

"Walk with me to Eden," he said.

He withdrew his hand. His fingers sought the handle of his coffee cup, and he sipped his coffee while watching me.

"And you can tell me everything," he continued. "You can tell me how you have worked with what we know, and what has happened since your return to Peru."

His words hung there over the table for an instant. There was no doubt then in my mind. There are certain opportunities that cannot be ignored; but more important, there are certain unconditional friends whose invitations must be accepted. *Eden?* I had no idea what he meant; Antonio was habitually subtle, but rarely cryptic.

And then the bubble burst. The owner of Los Marqueses was standing deferentially on the worn stone threshold of the café. She held an envelope in her hand, and when I looked up she pardoned herself and told me that I had received a telegram. It had arrived the day I left for the jungle, and she had been concerned because she had no idea when I would return. Behind her, Angelina was hiding, smiling toothlessly from around the corner of the doorjamb. She had seen my arrival and tattled to the Señora.

Only my office knew of my precise whereabouts, and knew that if I was using the hotel as a headquarters, a telegram was safer and more likely to reach me than a telephone message delivered in bad Spanish over crackling phone lines. I thanked the Señora and smiled at her until she excused herself. She pried Angelina from the doorjamb and crossed the street. I begged Antonio's pardon and tore open the envelope. It was from my mother via my office. My father was failing and I needed to fly to Miami.

I was not surprised, for his health had been declining steadily for the last year. I explained this to Antonio.

"It is an important thing. Critical," he said, "that you should attend to him."

He lifted the torn envelope from the checkered tablecloth and studied its front and back. "There is no greater way to honor another human being than by helping to set their spirit free from their body. And when it is a father, well, that is a sacred opportunity."

Una oportunidad sagrada, a sacred opportunity. Only Antonio would have paired those two words. He still held the envelope in his hand.

"When do you leave?" I asked, knowing that one opportunity had displaced the other, that while I was in Miami, my old friend would be walking alone.

"When you return," he said. "I will wait for you."

"But there is no telling how long I will be away. If he is dying it could take time. And there are family matters. . . . I can't ask you to wait indefinitely."

"You are not asking me," he said, simply. "I remember that you once waited for me, waited for the end of the school term so that I could show you the *altiplano.*"

"But you were doing me a favor," I replied.

"And you will do me a favor if you will accompany me," he said. "I would like your company on a trip that I must make alone."

He did not elaborate. I was so thrilled at the prospect of joining him, that I overlooked the strange contradiction of his request.

He set the envelope on the tablecloth in front of me. "Is this the envelope of your dream?"

It had not occurred to me. It wasn't the same—it was smaller and yellow—but it might just as well have been.

After all, it was only a dream.

12

Our noisy years seem moments in the being
Of the eternal Silence: truths that wake,
To perish never.

—*Wordsworth*

SO I LEFT WITH ALL MY QUESTIONS UNANSWERED,
and flew to Miami with the conviction of my experiences, but no explanation or interpretation.

Was any interpretation necessary?

Our behavior is guided and governed by our awareness. Our awareness is based on our sense experience—by the consensus of our senses.

We depend on five definable senses, six if we include the sense of intuition. I have spent most of my adult life working with altered aspects of these senses, learning to dream awake, to sense things in ways normally experienced when we are asleep, and to exercise the sixth sense; I can "see" light energies, perceive another's condition—sometimes their past and their future possibilities—know things automatically without learning them. All of these skills are by-products of a process that allows access to something like a conscious dream state. It is a process that can be catalyzed by rituals but is not dependent on them, a process that emphasizes the wisdom gained as well as the skills acquired in the realms of consciousness visited. In Huayna Picchu I had evidently acquired the skill to perceive from a point of view that was practically omniscient in its simultaneous use of my five senses. Could I label this multisensory perception as a seventh sense? Why not?

In the jungle I had acquired the ability, if not the skill (I did not know if I could control it, and, therefore, claim it as a skill) to perceive an abstract condition—humanity's impact on the environment—in a startlingly dramatic way.

So what had I learned? In Huayna Picchu, perhaps simply that there is an omniperceptual sense that operates in a realm that is to a dream what a dream is to waking consciousness. Then there was the incident with the condors, the eerie sensation of projecting myself into another body. This was a classic bit of shamanic lore: that one could become a power animal, acquire another form, and move through Nature with impunity. It had been demonstrated to me by this crone whom I had accompanied across the snow, although I did not understand it. I hardly trusted it.

And in the jungle? Why interpret what speaks for itself? I felt privileged to have lived through such a dramatization of my harmful effect on the Earth and the effect of my species. That such an ecological message would overwhelm me there still led me to wonder about the source of the experience. Surely that was no projection of my desires or preoccupations.

Flying 30,000 feet above the Earth, bound for Miami, I was forced in the wake of the incident in the jungle to admit that my sense of environmental responsibility had been until now unexceptional; I had never allowed my ecological awareness to inconvenience me.

May 1
Airborne

But if all of humanity could see what I saw and know what I know about this Earth as the home of our being for all time, how could we pursue policies of abuse? If we all knew that seventy-odd years was not an end to us, then it would be in our own self-interest to protect the world, to preserve it so that we could continue to use it. What matters if our motives are selfish then—as long as we stop the molestation?

And I do know that death is not an end to us. The concept of dying consciously, maintaining one's awareness after death, is fundamental to the shamanic traditions extant in every remote corner of the world. More than that, I had twice witnessed the freeing of an energy body from its vessel of flesh and bones: an old missionary woman Antonio attended, and El Viejo, Antonio's teacher, whose death I had formally attended. And now I hurtled toward Miami to do what I could for my father.

My anxiety was twofold: that I would be able to reach him, a man who knew nothing of what I believed. That a man so resistant to anything outside of the realm of his own pragmatic universe could be willing to follow my lead and let go. And then there was that other question. It had something to do with that young Indian who had twice crossed my path. It had something to do with Antonio's proposed expedition. But I was still unable to put the question into words. I was, I think, afraid of the answer.

I will try to paint a picture of what happened in Miami, how my father died, and what I did to help him. It is a part of this story because it has to do with my past and with death and with life in death, and it was the last thing that I did before completing the strange odyssey that I had begun when I traveled to Peru in search of Antonio.

My father was an attorney and businessman with a distinguished practice and a vigorous bank account. He was a dashing aristocrat, descended from a noble Spanish family, the son of an eclectic Catholic and devout capitalist physician who built his own hospital in the city of Havana, Cuba, in the 1920s. My father was a product of his privileged class and of his time: a stubborn, opinionated, and self-absorbed entrepreneur of the 1940s—a thoroughly intimidating figure with wavy hair and screen-idol features. His arrogance and determination led him to sue the Vatican for a divorce from his first wife. He married my mother a few years later. Like so many of his peers, he had underestimated the storm clouds of communism looming in the mountains of Cuba. He spent the second half of his life fighting to restore the fortune and the stature that he lost in December of 1959, when Castro seized the island and her banks and routed the rich and most of the middle class from their homeland. Although my father succeeded in restoring the family's economic equilibrium, he never quite recovered from his loss of country and faith.

Much could probably be made of my strained relationship with my father, but to what end? Popular therapy has, in the last few decades, successfully traced most of the neuroses that fret our culture back to dysfunctional parents and traumatic childhood episodes; I have worked through hundreds of such issues in my years of clinical practice. But by applying the primitive concept of the Earth and Sun as our progenitors, by emphasizing the child as a product of Nature rather than of dysfunctional parents, I had found that such pathologies healed rapidly. Patients and clients once impotent from all those deep-rooted vulnerabilities were empowered to love their parents in spite of their inadequacies. So, by practicing what I preached, I tended to discount the effect of my loveless relationship with my father, because I had resigned myself to it and found a way of respecting him and what he stood for. Three years past, when his health had started to fail him, my sister and I had thrown a surprise birthday party for him, and I had raised my glass to him. I remember how politely he had received my toast acknowledging the courage and audacity and richness that he had brought to his life.

For the past three years his health had gradually deteriorated; and consistent with longstanding tradition, my mother kept his condition a secret, even from him. She would not admit that he was dying, but would instead tend to his needs and love him with all her might and deny her present loss.

It is unnecessary to dwell on the clinical aspects of my father's death. Suffice it to say that his lungs were not absorbing enough oxygen. Although he could breath naturally, and was therefore unaware of the pathology, a large percentage of each breath was useless. His brain was deprived of a significant amount of oxygen and he would lapse, lose track of his thoughts, and simply fade away in the middle of a sentence.

And he was tired. When I arrived I found him in the living room, reclining asleep in his favorite chair. Thin, his character lines now wrinkles, he was an emaciated, still strikingly handsome caricature of himself. His hair was snow white and combed back from his temples in delicate waves. In spite of the fatigue that I had suffered in Peru, I felt awkwardly robust in his presence. There was oxygen in every room of the house, little heavy green cylinders with clear plastic tubes and opaque masks that covered the nose and mouth.

I sat with him that first afternoon while he slept, and listened to his breathing. When he opened his eyes he looked over at me and smiled.

"Why are you here?" he asked in his deep, mellifluous Spanish.

"I have come to be with you, *papi*," I said, matter-of-factly.

"Where have you been?"

"In Peru."

"Oh." He let his head fall back on the cushioned headrest. "Is your mother here?"

"No. She has gone to run an errand."

"We are here alone?"

"Yes."

Half an hour later he asked, "Is it time to eat?"

"No. But soon."

And later still he said, "Thank you for coming. Do you think that I am scared?"

"No," I said, "I do not think that you are scared. But if you are, we are here."

We spoke for nearly twenty minutes. He was fully aware of what was happening to him. He spoke about himself, and vaguely about the years that he worked so hard to milk opportunity. "I am not a bad man," he said, "but I have not been good at everything that I have done. I have not been able to do everything that I wanted to do. And you will take good care of your mother."

Of course I would. I realized that he was saying good-bye to me the moment he began to speak.

"I love you, *papi*," I said.

Just before he closed his eyes and returned to his dreams, he said: "I know that you can help me."

And that was how he told me that he loved me. In that moment of acknowledgment, he gave me something that I had waited for my whole life.

He had always known of my work, and had perfected an air of judgmental politeness when listening to my descriptions of my experiences and theories. But I did not know that he had ever read one of my books. I still do not know for a fact that he ever did. But he asked for my help; he whispered his respect for me and put himself in my hands, opened himself to me; and although we were never able to share his life, we were able to share his leaving it.

We began that very evening. I got up in the middle of the night and entered his bedroom, where the curtains held the moonlight; their ghostly glow and the orange nightlight were the only light. I gripped the cold chrome bar of the rented hospital bed and leaned over and kissed him on the forehead. Then I softened my focus and looked at the swirls of dull dry light that marked his chakras, and proceeded to disengage them one at a time.

The Hindus were among the first to document the existence of the seven energy centers of the human body, the respiratory system of the energy body. The first is at the base of the spine, at the genitals; the second is slightly below the navel; the third is the pit of the stomach, at the solar plexus; the fourth is at the center of the chest, at the heart, the fifth is at the base of the throat; the sixth is above and between the eyebrows; and the seventh is at the top of the head. Physiologically each corresponds to nerve bundles or plexuses along the spine and with the seven major endocrine glands. I first learned to "see" them in the early 1970s during my stay with an urban healer and his wife on the outskirts of Cuzco. It was they who had first trained me to "see with my eyes closed," and I have maintained the skill for many years, seeing energy bodies, the so-called auras, and the chakras—delicate little vortices of light, right-handed spirals of energy spinning clockwise and discernible with a softened gaze focused an inch above the surface of the body.

So I disengaged them; with my index and middle fingers together, I spun them counterclockwise, one at a time and watched my father sink into a profound and relaxed sleep—from which he awoke, startled. His breathing accelerated; the change in rhythm caught me while I was dozing in an armchair, and I snapped awake and watched him surface from his dream. He called my name and told me that they had come for him. "I could not come back!" he whispered to me, inches from my face; he was not panicked, but amazed that he had seen anything so wonderful as whoever it was who had come for him, and surely frightened of the sensation of going somewhere whence he could not return. "I am scared," he told me, sometime before dawn.

For the next two weeks we worked for an hour or so every day before he napped. He sat reclined in his armchair in the living room and closed his eyes, and I guided our meditation together. Together, for I had become accustomed to taking myself to places in my mind, feeling the freedom to let myself go, knowing that I could return at will from my self-induced state. My goal was to bring him with me. So I sat beside him and closed my eyes and spoke softly, guiding the experience until it took on a life of its own.

We "went" to a river. I said:

"Come with me to the riverbank, and see how the sharp ridge of sand at the water's edge gives way under the pressure of our shoes and the wet sand tumbles into the water and makes a little cloud and joins the sand of the riverbed. Here, hold my hand. Listen to the sound of the water rippling over the rocks so smooth and shiny in the crystal-clear stream flowing around the bend where the leaves of the ash and poplar trees are shimmering in the sun or hidden in the shadows. Leaves so healthy and green and full of life, they look waxed and they shine in the sunlight. Summertime, and the air is so clean and crisp that it fills your sinus and clears your head with every inhalation. Breathe. In. Deeply. And exhale and look across the river to the other side, the bank of sand and rocks and pebbles bleached white in the sun, and, back a ways . . . a line of tall trees and then the green hillside sloping up and away. There are rocks downstream on our side; we will walk downstream to them, but not so near the river's edge, because our shoes sink deep and send clumps of wet sand into the water, so we will walk a few feet from the water and here, take my hand . . . we can sit on this rock together. Find a comfortable place and unlace your shoes and roll down your socks and let's look down into the water and see what we can see. I love the way the sunlight glistens silver-white flashes of light where the sun touches the water. . . ."

And on, and on, simple words, familiar images that eventually conspired to create a place for us to be together. For the first few days he listened and fell asleep to the sound of my voice, low and steady, never faltering for an instant, that I might paint a picture of a constant place. He would drift off and I would sit in quiet mediation with him, fixing the place in my mind's eye. It became an exercise, and when I was with him I forgot that he was my father.

Then one afternoon in the middle of our meditation, my father smiled and murmured: "The water is very clear. I can see the bottom." And then he fell asleep.

That night he saw things, beautiful, translucent people who were talking to him, but he could not remember in the morning what it was that they said.

Then one day, a week later—it was another afternoon—he saw me, sitting on the rock by the water.

"There you are," he said. And I saw him standing there in the sand. He saw me and I saw him looking at me. A light breeze actually lifted a few strands of his hair and he was younger; I was seeing him as he saw himself, in that ideal, most flattering vision we hold of ourselves. He was wearing baggy linen trousers and a cotton shirt and his face was tanned and healthy.

It was such a delicate moment, together in our consensual reality of our dream time, and that fleeting image I had of him smiling up at me where I waited for him on the rock by the water overwhelmed me. I opened my eyes and he was lying back with his head on a cushion and a grin on his dry, colorless lips, and the sight of him wavered as tears stung my eyes.

"Where have you gone?" he mumbled. He called my name and I closed my eyes and tried so hard to get back to those rocks where he stood looking for me, but my tears just broke and slid down my cheeks and I had lost it, lost all concentration. Mercifully, he fell asleep.

Working so hard to help him to die, I found myself yearning for him to live. I slept alone that night and cried for him and for me and for every moment lost between us. We will do anything to avoid pain, we try so desperately to sidestep the agonies in our quest for the ecstasies that we miss out on the lessons of pain, the growth that we experience when we hurt. If nothing else, the endorsement of our humanness, the stamp of sentience that deep emotion embosses on our being ought to be precious to us, for the more we learn genuinely to feel, the closer we approach the omnisensory state where wisdom waits for us.

We had made a breakthrough. He had learned to see in a different realm and I had learned to feel the love that loss reveals. We had finally met.

We spent a great deal of time there on the rocks beside that pastoral stream, in the late afternoons before he left me for his dreams, nodded off, and wandered in his own spaces. He would describe to me what we saw together, whisper to me the things that we both saw floating by:

We saw debris—leaves, and tangles of branches, flower petals, even.

We saw people floating downstream past the rock where we sat together. Some I recognized, others he identified for me: friends and relatives, some still living, most of them long dead. Sometimes I would see nothing there but hear his voice speaking to them, telling me who they were and what they had been to him. And this is how I came to know more about my father than I had before—from the vague figures that were sometimes only an impression to me, but were evident and visible to him on those afternoons and evenings when we visited the river. Some, he said, were saying good-bye, and others were telling him to follow.

We never spoke about these times; there was no formal acknowledgment of the phenomenon that we shared, and none was needed. I would simply sit with him and guide his breathing and lull him back with my description, and he would lock in and fade out; and only later, with a look or a whimsical smile, when he awoke and ate a little supper, sitting almost listlessly by the table, would he acknowledge our journeys together.

But that is how I remember him—as he saw himself, a handsome man in his potency: a man who lunched with presidents; lawyer, builder, entrepreneur, a good provider, an uninvolved father, a man who sat with me on a rock by a summer stream and told me of his life.

Then one morning he suffered a seizure that left him in a coma. He was rushed to the hospital where, in a corner room, alone with my mother, he died. My sister and I had gone out to bring back some food, and when we returned, his face was relaxed in that perfect stillness of death.

My sister burst into tears and I dropped the bag of food and went to him and began to disengage the faint, still fading, slowly swirling seven spirals. Automatically, oblivious to my mother's sobs and my sister's weeping anguish, I went to his feet and pushed the emergent energy body, faintly glowing at his chest, out through his throat, saw its milky luminescence ascend, then withdraw back into the body. Again, I repeated the process. Working as Antonio had worked, with eyes half-closed, I disengaged his chakras—now colorless, like faint swirls in the sand—and pushed from his feet, and it rose again, amorphous, translucent, like an opal with no specific shape, and his aura collapsed—like the husks of plants in the dead jungle of my Amazon vision—no light was there to outline his form, and I sealed the chakras, in a ceremonial gesture of closing the body to the light that animates it. And when I opened my eyes, he was gone.

All that remained was an echo in my mind, his words, his voice: "I am not afraid."

And late that night, when I returned to our spot by the river, I was alone on the rock, and the water flowed clear. And I realized that we had met only to say good-bye.

13

Past the near meadows, over the still stream
Up the hill-side; and now 'tis buried deep
In the next valley-glades:
Was it a vision, or a waking dream?

—John Keats

"DURING THE CHURCH SERVICE THE NEXT MORN-
ing, something happened, and it was remarkable, although I didn't trust it
then and I'm not sure that I trust it now. There were over a hundred people there—the pews were full.

"I . . . had no emotion left; I was wrung out—we all were: My mother
was exhausted and probably still in shock—her tears were all shed—and my
sister was still grieving. And I had spent time—time that he had never had
for me—with a father who had been a stranger to me. We had shared that
rock together—witnessed his lifetime together beside the river. In the space
of two weeks, I had acquired so much history with the man. And then lost
him. And I had helped him to die, to leave the world alive.

"And I was sitting there on the hard wooden pew beside my mother.
The church service wore on and soon there was the silence of prayer for
my father, and I must have lapsed into some sort of altered state. While ev-
eryone, friends and family, directed their prayers and thoughts to my father, I was staring straight ahead, unfocused, toward the closed casket, and

it was as though I saw . . ." The memory of what I was about to describe hovered in my imagination, where it had been summoned by the story I told. I had not intended to tell him this part.

Antonio stopped. We had crossed a small stream, an irrigation ditch spanned by a sort of sod-covered bridge of very old logs. All along the banks where the water trickled were bursts of narrow-blade grass browning in the summer heat.

"Yes?" he said, expectantly. "What did you see?"

"Nothing that I am sure of," I said. "There are so many other things to talk about."

He sat on an arbitrary pile of stones there by the stream. He leaned forward and rested his elbows on his knees and clasped his hands. I should never have faltered; I had created unintentional suspense.

"It was an impression, that's all. I thought that it was the . . . what? The energy? The manifestation of their thoughts and prayers? Like a sort of dim pastel vortex of light that turned along the length of the aisle, and its eye, the focal point of all this spinning phenomenon was somewhere near the casket, but not *at* it."

"Did you feel your father there in the church?" he asked. He raised his head to watch me answer, and the shadow cast by his hat brim lifted from his face and stopped on his forehead, and his eyes captured the light of the low Sun, and I saw that the mahogany brown of his irises was made of many colors.

"I don't know," I said. "I sensed him, I think. I'm reluctant to say— maybe up there at the focal point near the casket. But I was exhausted."

I sighed and gazed off across the *altiplano,* toward the faintly snow-brushed Andes piled up on the far horizon. He squinted at me. "You have seen so much in your years. Why do you discount this experience in the church?"

"I was tired."

"Some of the most magnificent things are seen when the body is spent and the brain is quiet."

"Also," I said, "I would *like* to know that the focused thought of a prayer can have a form, can be received . . ."

"To know that your father was regaining his integrity, his wholeness in the state that he had entered?" He opened his little cloth bag and his hand felt for something inside. "That he was disoriented and awkward, like a child taking its first unsteady steps in a new world, and the prayers of his friends and family helped him somehow?"

I nodded and accepted the stick of rolled cinnamon bark that he offered me from his pouch.

"But you prefer to disregard your vision because it could be a manifestation of something that you *want* to believe."

"No," I said, carefully. "I prefer to think that what I perceived was commonplace—the phenomenon if not the ability to perceive it. But I don't *know* it. I was tired and susceptible to seeing what I wanted to see. The conditions were all wrong. I want very much to believe that love can be such a tangible thing, that it is malleable and can be concentrated, directed, that it can make a difference. But I would never describe that vision in the church to anyone, because I wanted it too much. I was exhausted and I had lost my objectivity."

"So," he said. "While you continue your work of the Medicine Wheel and document your adventures, you have become judgmental of your experiences. You have learned the responsibility that this path requires, and you are anxious to set an example for others who might follow. So you edit your experiences for fear that if any one of them is discounted, they all will be discarded."

He pushed himself up from the pile of rocks, and we proceeded across the plateau and toward a tree line some miles away. We walked on as though we had never broken our stride.

"Responsibility?" I said. "Yes. It's easy to describe my work to people who are willing to believe—then it's simply a matter of telling the truth; the challenge and the responsibility is to engage those whose minds have been made up for them and set in concrete —" I glanced over at him. He had placed his hand on my shoulder as we dropped down into the dry bed of a shallow *arroyo*.

"Look," I said. "What you know and what I have learned—the things that we have faith in are those things that we have experienced directly. In my culture there is very little time for people to explore and discover for themselves. Time is money, and money buys time, and balance is a dollar figure in the lower right-hand corner of a bank statement. Up there—" I cocked my head to the north—"what is known is based on scientifically or legally established fact. My culture is spiritually bankrupt."

I shoved the cinnamon stick back into the corner of my mouth and chewed on it.

"Do not be angry."

"I'm not angry."

"Impatient, then."

He had me there. I frowned and tried to connect all of this angst—this spasm of frustration—with my story of the morning after my father's death.

Of all of the things that I wanted so desperately to describe to him, my experience on the morning after my father's death was the least important. I had worked so long to maintain the balance between the subjective and objective aspects of my developing perceptions. I knew when the conditions were right, and that subtle vision in the church was suspect. And it was private. I could choose to believe in it or not; it was not subject to discussion, but Antonio had fixed on it. He had drawn me out, coaxed me to recount my experience of my father's death down to the last detail.

And here I was rambling on about the perversion of religion that had obscured the principles of spirituality and created the apathy, cynicism, and amorality that plague modern society.

Then it made sense, suddenly. Whatever his reasons for pressing me about Miami, Antonio had led me to define my discomfort. And I felt it then, the pain of it in my chest, the burden of it, this abstract fact, this manifesto that formed itself like an embolism, empty in itself, exerting an awful pressure. And there was the self-consciousness of it, the gnawing of self-importance and self-appointed responsibility. It was simply this: that if what I learn is important, if it is of any consequence that a contemporary man can experience profound states of consciousness that are believed to belong exclusively to the mystics and saints and madmen of ancient history, then it *must* be communicated. Truthfully, clearly, without compromise. It was not the burden of proof, but the burden of truth that I was carrying;

and at the moment when I realized this I also knew that it did not matter, so long as I was true. Others could manufacture doubt and pick over my tale with the sharp, sterile implements of skepticism, and integrity was my only defense. I thought this at the time; what I said was: "Why describe something that I am unsure of when I am sure of so much?"

He nodded as though he understood this perfectly, had felt it himself, and managed to come to terms with it. We walked in silence for a few minutes, a long while, then he said: "You did not wish to tell me about this because you doubt it. But there comes a time when we accept the information of our senses without prejudice. It is not necessary to compromise the experience by qualifying it."

"Maybe not to you," I said, "but try describing such things to someone whose faith is ready-made and whose sense of reality is practically legislated."

"Discretion must be used when you recount these things. I was not criticizing you, my friend, but observing that in editing the experiences of your senses for the sake of truth, you have become a storyteller."

I could not help but laugh at this. It was one of those involuntary moments when you feel joy, when delight shivers through your body and you can almost taste contentment. I was in Peru in body and spirit, walking cross-country with my old friend by whose side I had learned so much, and it was as though we had never broken our stride. He smiled back at me.

"But whether or not you chose ever to tell that particular incident," he said, grinning, "it is beautiful thing and worth believing."

Although my return to Peru is accomplished with the turning of a page, a full two months had passed since my father's death. I had stayed in Miami to attend to family affairs and traveled to California to secure a new home for a new family. All the while, my mind's eye was on Peru.

So it was mid-July when we left Cuzco and once again set out for the high plateau of central Peru on what was to be the first and shortest leg of a ten-day journey to Eden. We had taken the train, third class, for quite a ways before disembarking at a rural station and retracing steps we had taken fifteen years before—a half-day's trek to a little hill in the middle of a meadow.

The long dry season had claimed the *altiplano;* the rugged expanse of granite-studded pastures and deep *arroyos* and stunted shrubs was all straw yellow and orange and brick red where the soil was upturned by a *campesino*'s plow or a burrowing animal. Here and there, granite-crested hills and barren little troughs of valleys relieved the monotony of the plains; an occasional forest of pine trees or eucalyptus made irregular patches of dark green between the white-blue sky and the flaxen landscape.

I was doing fine, traveling light, exhilarated by Antonio's company and the clean, dry, precious air 11,000 feet above sea level. Professor Morales was in high spirits. He moved as gracefully as ever, although I detected something determined, methodical in his gait. He wore his country clothes: light wool trousers, lace-up boots that supported his ankles, a blousey raw cotton shirt and modest brown poncho; he wore another fedora, older, with the salty outlines of sweat stains permanently impregnated in the satin band. The little cloth bag was hanging from a braided cord on his shoulder, and contained his sticks of cinnamon bark, yucca paste, cornmeal, and perhaps some coca leaves.

Our destination was a knoll in the middle of a meadow near a small forest of pine trees. There is a modest ruin on the crest of the hill, a pile of stones cut and worn into blocks by Inca masons many centuries ago. The foundation of the ruin is half-buried in red soil and long brown grass. Perhaps the walls were wrecked by the Spanish as an exercise—target practice for one of His Majesty's artillery pieces—and the stones were dragged off, appropriated by scavenging *campesinos* over hundreds of years. It might have been an observation post, or a storehouse, a *tambo,* one of the hundreds that linked the Inca Empire. Now it is nothing but a pile of scattered stones, a child's toppled tower of building blocks. The foundation is roughly square, and one corner, the far corner, is higher than the other four. Fifteen years ago I had stood up on that corner wall and looked down the far side of the hill to the valley of sharp shadows and warm colors in the slanting rays of a low Sun. It was here that I had first engaged in ritual with Antonio. Having just discovered that Professor Antonio Morales of Cuzco was don Jicaram of the *altiplano,* I had listened for the first time to his invocation of the spirits of the Four Winds. It was the evening after the revelation of his identity. I had watched him free the spirit of a dying missionary woman, and we had come here to fetch his *mesa.* That was the beginning of our adventures together. Now in our beginning is our end, so here we had returned on the same errand to bring an end to something. I hardly knew then the shape that end would take.

Once again we walked through a gap in the foundation wall and made for a large, expertly cut stone that lay nestled beside the wall of that corner enclosure. We turned it over together—it took all of our strength—to expose the rock-lined hole eight inches deep, a foot wide, two feet long, and the long bundle that fit so perfectly in the space.

We had gathered firewood on our way to the ruin, and we stacked a traditional four-sided framework of the twigs and sticks, stuffed brittle grass in the center, and sparked it off as the Sun set over the plateau.

I watched the old professor unroll the threadbare brown-and-red woven Inca cloth and set out the objects of his *mesa* with quiet precision. Antonio's collection of power objects was simple and elegant: a short, dark hardwood staff carved with a left-hand spiral, another of polished bone with a handle like an eagle's beak—these represented polarity, the pair of opposites, light and dark. From a pouch he withdrew a piece of carved obsidian—an Inca-style griffin, half-jaguar, half-bird—representing the Earth and the sky. A dolphin carved fancifully from some exotic wood, a ceramic hermaphrodite, stone figures inlaid with abalone shell, a shard of crystal, a necklace of opalescent stones, and other things, fetishes worn smooth with that peculiar quality of things treasured and handled for centuries. My owl, the little gold owl, had come from this collection through which don Jicaram engaged with the forces of Nature. I scooped it out of my pocket and placed it on the spread cloth, then sat back and watched Antonio.

He sat there with the rosy glow of the sunset and the pastel orange light of the fire illuminating his face from different angles. He sat and caressed each figure with his eyes. And then he invoked the Four Winds.

When he was through it all, when the power had been summoned, the spirits allied, when the very atmosphere of the hill had been sanctified to serve our purpose, he sat down across from me.

"Please," he said, "tell me the story."

And I told him everything, recounted the steps of my solo return to Peru—the steps that led to our meeting in the café on Calle Garcilaso. It took hours; I do not know how many. He kept the fire stoked, and the stars that showed on the horizon were high and sparkling in the night sky when I concluded. I started with my dreams of the cat-and-mouse game through the Andes, the "first story ever told," which began as an exercise with the group in Canyon de Chelly. I told him about the stolen gold of the Lord of Sipan, described my return to Cuzco, the encounter with the *pischaco*, the undead thing at Sacsayhuaman, my determination to hike the Inca Trail.

He was leaning close to the fire; closer to catch every word as I described my discovery of the young Indian in the Valley of the Rainbows and the subject of our dialogues as we made our way to Machu Picchu and his unexpected departure.

"It was late in the afternoon—there was not much light left, but he went anyway. He walked away, headed through the ruins, and disappeared over the side of the hill."

"And he said?"

" 'I am going to Vilcabamba.' "

Antonio sat back, leaned away from the fire as though the words pushed him away. Although his expression remained fixed and passive, I knew that he was impressed with this.

I detailed my vision of the dancers before the Pachamama Stone, and the little girl who led me to climb Huayna Picchu in the dark, in the rain. I did my best to relate the perceptions and sensations of my dream-space visit with the crone who lived in the snowbound peak, tried to express that omnisensory state. His eyes were dancing in the firelight. Elbows on knees, fingers steepled as though in prayer, forefingers touching his lips, he listened the way one listens to a favorite piece of music.

He laughed, delighted by my confusion on waking in the cave on the side of the mountain.

Then I took him through the jungle, my brush with the *Sendero,* the overwhelming anguish of the dying Earth and my determination to put an end to it all.

And I realized in the telling that the anxiety that I had carried with me, my need for and anticipation of his answers to all of my questions, had disappeared. Who was my young friend of the Inca Trail? How did he know the story that I had made up? What had happened to me at Huayna Picchu? What was this dizzy new state of consciousness that I had entered? Who was that woman, that crone? What was it that had mutated the jungle that I saw into a Golgotha, a garden of agony and death? What was it that led me to safety? He appeared to me as my friend of the Inca Trail, but the Campas saw a jaguar, an old one. Why did I return to Peru in the first place? Why have I persistently put myself through all of this?

It was the story itself that was important, as though everything that I had seen and thought and felt was meant simply to be told. My need to understand had been consumed by the fire little by little, with every combustible word I uttered or metaphor I spun. A greater need had been at once revealed and relieved: my need to tell the story.

It was not until that night when I shed the burden of my questions that I realized how taxed I had forever been by my own experiences. Suddenly, staring into the embers of the fire that Antonio was now allowing to die, I knew that in twenty years, although I had discovered new ways of experiencing myself and my world, I had yet to discover a new way of *understanding* the experiences of my senses—that I had agonized over explanations of what I knew and how I had come to know it all, and I had applied all the facilities of my rational mind to make my adventures conform to reason, correspond to a logically uniform system of thought from which I could glean no wisdom—when all that I had to do was to tell a story that conformed to truth, corresponded to fact. It is not necessary for the story-teller to understand fully the meaning of what is told, only to tell the truth.

So the explanations were unimportant now. And perhaps because I no longer needed to feel satisfied, Antonio set out to provide me with everything that I needed to know.

He wasted no time. We began the next morning. By the time we were finished, I knew the meaning of my story, and I knew the meaning of his.

PART IV

JOURNEY
TO THE ISLAND
OF THE SUN

14

Ere the blabbing eastern scout,
The nice Morn on th' Indian steep
From her cabin'd loop-hole peep.

—*John Milton*

I WOKE WITH A SPASM IN MY GUT, DOUBLED OVER,
cramped into a fetal position in my sleeping bag, my back hard against the
granite wall of the ruin. Antonio was squatting by the gray ash remains of
our fire, molding balls of yucca and corn paste for breakfast. Surreptitiously
I chewed a couple of Bactrim and prayed that my stomach would not be-
tray me, that the *turista* that follows nearly every border crossing north to
south *and* south to north would not disable me. The *altiplano* was unfamiliar, its character softened and obscured by morning fog. And it was
cold; I should have packed a sweater. But the Sun, cresting the jagged horizon, would soon sweep the fog and the chill from the fields; a little food and
the long walk back would settle my stomach.

After a hasty breakfast of yucca and corn and dried mango slices, we
set off for Cuzco, headed back the way we had come. Antonio carried his
mesa wrapped in its cloth and slung over his shoulder like a quiver of arrows. It was midday when we reached the rural train station and another
two hours waiting for the train, and I could not hide my misery. My in-
testines were writhing and I barely endured the two-hour third-class train
ride to Cuzco. I did the best I could to sleep, to calm my stomach and my
impatience with the medicine, but the train stopped wherever there were

people standing by the tracks. In the country of the *altiplano* the train is like an urban trolley; its passengers—the farmers and their children—commute from one obscure stop to another. There were the goats and pigs and chickens, gray burlap and nylon mesh bags of grain and corn, worn wooden crates of soda, infants wrapped and bound to their mothers by colorful *mantas;* and when there were not enough seats, when the aisle was crammed with passengers, Antonio insisted that we stand, yield our wooden seat or bench to a woman or an old man. I was dying to reach Cuzco before I lost control of myself, and I am sure that I paled under my sunburn when Antonio indicated that we were getting off at a suburban station one or two stops from the city.

"I know that you are feeling foul, my friend," he said as the train pulled away and left us standing on the outskirts of a poor semirural neighborhood, "but we must see someone before we go. She will cure your stomach and cleanse both of us for tomorrow's departure. We have come so far together, it is important that we go step by step now. It is only half a mile or so."

"Where do we go tomorrow?"

"To Puno," he said. "On the shore of Lake Titicaca. There is a place that you must see before we find Eden." He grinned at me. "But I must ask you to clear your mind for this meeting. My friend is from *la ceja de selva,* "the brow of the jungle," the region that lies between Paucartambo and Madre de Dios. She is a 'long-hair,' a Q'ero Indian. I have known her from when I was a child. She was the daughter of a *hatun laika*—"

"Wait a moment," I said, and stopped in the dusty street all russet orange in the afternoon light. "You are Q'ero?"

"Yes."

This was news to me. It had always been enough that he was Quechua and the only native Indian on the faculty of the National University of Cuzco. But that he was Q'ero, a "long-hair," was stunning.

In 1955 a group of Peruvian anthropologists, ethnologists, geographers, and sundry specialists mounted an expedition into the region between the highland and the jungle to study these natives who were, until then, untouched by modern civilization, forgotten by history. I knew the head of that expedition, Dr. Oscar Nuñez del Prado, and its chief archaeologist, Dr. Manuel Chavez Ballon; I had heard them describe the tribe who lived on the "brow of the jungle" and farmed a vertical zone from the 5,000-foot-high forests to the glacial zones above 14,000 feet. Their lives are spent in a perpetual cycle of climbing and descending, from the lowland forests to the highland peaks and back, cultivating and harvesting the crops that they have perfected in each zone. They speak a pure Quechua, unadulterated by Spanish. Their shamanic practices are legendary, based on a principle called *ayni,* a sort of reciprocity between humans and Nature.

A self-sufficient society living in isolation in a remote and wild region of Peru. A poor people by any modern standard, invisible to the rest of the world. Dr. Nuñez del Prado had "discovered" them by accident; at a fiesta in the town of Paucartambo in 1949, his attention was drawn to several humble farmers whose comportment was so dignified that it distinguished them from the rest. Six years later he mounted an expedition into the hazardous *ceja de selva.* The results of this exploration were documented in newspapers and anthropological journals and forgotten by all but a handful of academics.

So Antonio was Q'ero. "I didn't know," I said.

He smiled and shrugged. "Is it important?"

"How did you come to Cuzco?"

"I walked. This woman," he nodded, indicating our destination, "told me that I should go to the city and find the priests and learn what they knew."

We walked in silence past the *tiendas* and open doorways, the dogs and the chickens and the half-naked children playing. This was more of his personal history than he had ever disclosed. I knew that he had studied with a master shaman in order to become a *hatun laika* himself. I had been present on the occasion of El Viejo's death in his modest adobe *casita* on the edge of a pine tree thicket somewhere on the *altiplano.* I wanted to hear more. He continued without prompting.

"One of the priests, Father Diego, would often take the story of Christ with him on walks across the *altiplano.* It was with him that I met El Viejo. I was fifteen or sixteen. I went to school in Cuzco . . ." He trailed off. His memories were catching up to him. The past had so little bearing on his present, I suspect that he had not thought about his personal history for years. "Well," he resumed, "I could not pay for school. The priests taught me all that I needed to know to go to the university."

"How did you avoid becoming a Catholic?"

"I spent all my free time working, doing chores, cleaning, sweeping out the churches of Cuzco. But I would leave for months at a time. I told them I had to return to visit my family, but I went instead to visit El Viejo. I always came back and the priests trusted me. I was the Indian boy, but I was honest and curious. The priests saw to my formal education and instructed me in the teachings of Christ. El Viejo showed me things that helped me to understand my Indian origins and see the priests as re-tellers of a story that they had not written—a story of one man's experience of the Divine."

His pace had slowed perceptibly and temporarily I forgot the turmoil in my guts, so eager was I to hear his story. I had never thought of Antonio as anything but my elder—so it is with parents and teachers.

"I learned," he said, "that religions are simple concepts of spirituality—values, standards, truths, *principles* communicated in the form of a story that uses poetry and metaphor to illustrate its wisdom. Stories that have been told and retold until even their embellishments acquire profound meaning and the figurative is taken literally and the lessons are lost. And my friends, the priests, were devoted caretakers of a story that was not their own." He was smiling at the ground.

"But the shaman is the author of the story, the mythmaker. El Viejo's faith was based on his own experience of the Divine in Nature. A shaman stands with one foot in this world and one foot in the world of spirit. With the priests and in the schools, I learned the lessons of others. With El Viejo I learned my own lessons.

"El Viejo showed me what you also have learned, that the consciousness that creates our waking reality is a universal consciousness, a vast sea that is navigable. Most people are content to live on the land, and they know this sea only as it appears to them from their own shores. But it is possible to know it fully, to navigate the sea, to cross it, to immerse yourself, to let it wash over you, to discover its depths. The shaman is one who has learned how to swim and how to sail, how to navigate through this sea and return to its shores. And to communicate its wonders to his people."

We had turned into a narrow street with an open gutter and an uneven sidewalk of smooth flagstones. A row of painted doors were set into a long wall of adobe, from which layers of sand and lime stucco had been cracking and chipping for a hundred years. Antonio stopped and turned to me.

"So you see, I have led a double life for all of my life."

"One foot in and one foot out," I said.

"If you like." He placed his hand on my arm. "This woman is La Mascadora de la Coca. She also lives in two worlds. She is very wise and very . . . accomplished. You have met her before. She sat beside you during the vigil for El Viejo's death. The old woman who passed the pipe to you?" I nodded. "She is much older, now, of course, but I think that you will recognize her. She speaks no Spanish."

La Mascadora de la Coca, "she who chews coca," lived in a nondescript whitewashed adobe house with a plain wooden door at the end of the street where all of the doors were painted. Antonio and I spent the night with her, then flagged down a taxi idling on the outskirts of the suburb and got back to Cuzco and the Hotel los Marqueses at five A.M. I had to bang Antonio's walking stick on the studded double wooden doors to wake the doorman. I showered, threw some warm clothes into a daypack to supplement my fanny pack, and left my bags in front of the Señora's door with a note asking her to store them safely, that I would settle my bill on my return. The train for Puno left at seven A.M. It was on time. I was dog-tired, but I would not rest until I had committed to paper the events of the last three days and two nights.

July 6

Something is happening. It feels like acceleration, as if the clock is ticking faster than before.

The Cuzco-Puno train, the most wretched ride in Peru. We are traveling third class, naturally. Writing in this student notebook that I picked up in Cuzco because I left my journal in California. No tray tables—writing on my lap. This is the first chance I've had to digest what has happened and what is happening.

Three days ago Antonio and I returned to the place where he keeps his *mesa*, a hill by the edge of the *altiplano*. I had no idea what he had in mind. I decided to travel light—strapped my sleeping bag to a fanny pack containing the basics and a clean pair of socks.

We got to the ruin just before sunset, built a fire, and Antonio laid out his *mesa* and performed a simple invocation. And the sum total of our work that night was the telling of my adventures. I told him the whole story from Canyon de Chelly to Cuzco, the Inca Trail, Huayna Picchu, the jungle.

He interrupted only once, to ask what exactly my companion said to me before he left me at Machu Picchu.

By the time I finished the story it was late. We were both tired. Antonio closed our circle and that was that. I went to sleep in a corner of the ruin and felt a satisfaction that I have never known—as though by telling the story, I had dispossessed myself of the burden of understanding it, the responsibility of defining it, of making sense of the experiences of my senses.

When I fell asleep I had no idea of what he thought about it all, only that he had heard me, that it was important to him as well.

I awoke with gut-wrenching cramps. Sick as a dog. It took us all day to get back to Cuzco, but we didn't go to Cuzco, we stopped to see a friend of Antonio's, a Q'ero Indian woman (I have learned that Antonio is Q'ero), La Mascadora de la Coca, a shamaness who lives in a simple home on the outskirts of Cuzco and "exists" also in a hut on the snowbound peak of one of the great *apus*.

She was the old crone whom I met ten or twelve years ago when El Viejo died.

And she is the woman of my dream-time excursion in Huayna Picchu.

—We've taken on some more passengers. A bumpy piece of track now—an Indian woman as wide as the aisle and carrying two bags of *quinoa* is heading this way—a six-year-old girl behind her with a baby strapped to her back. Antonio looks at me and I can see it coming . . .

saved by a little boy three rows up. He surrendered his seat. Antonio grins.—

She barely glanced at me, La Mascadora, when she opened the door. The streaked gray hair with the one long side-braid tied with ribbon, the horribly wrinkled face and scant eyebrows and smoldering black eyes. It was she, there is no doubt about it. She wore a simple cotton dress that looked ridiculous—she belongs in layers of wool skirts and shawls—she belongs in the snow or in the orange light of her own lard candles. Her lips and teeth are stained with *llibta* (she smiled at Antonio), and if he has known her since he left the *ceja de selva* and she is the one who told him to go, she must be at least ten years his senior. She would be in her mid- to late nineties. It was a two-room house, a large living room and a kitchen. There were palm mats on the packed dirt floor and a few pieces of wooden furniture. There was evidently no electricity—only oil lamps and candles that would be lit soon. In the kitchen area there was a counter covered with herb bundles and bottles and vials of every sort. There was a rickety old army cot and a large clay oven, that she called a *huatia,* like those used to cook potatoes—igloo-shaped with a hole in the top.

Antonio had brought a bottle of *pisco* and a small bag of coca leaves, traditional gifts, and La Mascadora accepted them and opened the bottle and poured out a capful and tipped it to let a few drops dribble to the bare earth floor as a *pago,* an offering to the Pachamama. Then she offered the cap to Antonio, who toasted the two of us and drank, then passed it to me. The sweet, clear liquor burned all the way down, and I felt it hit my stomach and I tried to hide the shudder and the nausea that welled up in my throat. I passed it to La Mascadora. She drank, then proceeded to wrap the coca leaves around chunks of lime-clay *llibta,* and there we sat around her table, chewing coca and drinking *pisco* while she and Antonio spoke pure Quechua. The bitter juice of the coca and *llibta* was numbing my mouth and revolting my stomach. I could hardly follow their chatter, though I caught a few words, including

Titicaca. And I caught the fierceness in her ember eyes a few times when she glanced at me.

After the *pisco* had made a few rounds, she went to the kitchen and I saw her pump up a little Primus stove. Antonio explained that she was going to prepare us for our journey, cleanse us, and incidentally cure my stomach.

The next thing I know I am crammed into the clay oven, naked, hunched over, hugging my knees to my chest, my head sticking out through the hole. She has set a pressure cooker on the Primus, and a rubber tube leads from the nipple on the sealed lid to the inside of the oven. The pressure cooker is whistling and the oven is filling with pungent steam I recognize as *toé*—she has filled the pressure cooker with water and the branches, leaves, and blossoms of the datura plant. The oven is a sauna.

I squat there, tucked into the oven for what must have been an hour while Antonio and the woman sit at the table and chew coca and gossip. The thickness of the steam and the heat of it, the pungency of its odor, and the claustrophobic little oven are almost unbearable. I feel the *toé* steam cleansing my pores, but know that I am surely absorbing the essence of the plant through my skin, inhaling the steam deep into my lungs, and I start to feel giddy.

Then she is in the room, pouring a spoonful of white liquid from an amber glass bottle. Antonio steps in and explains that this is *toé* extract, for internal and external purification.

Just what I need. I begin to suspect that they are having a grand time putting me through all of this. I am sweating profusely and the steam is prickly, as though I have been rolling around in a bed of poison ivy. I could lose control of my stomach at any moment, and here I am taking datura. I remind myself to pop another Bactrim.

—It's freezing in this train. The morning fog or mist is still lingering ghostlike over the *altiplano*.—

Another ten minutes pass, then La Mascadora is standing behind me, holding my head in her hands and singing softly in a dialect that I do not recognize, but the cadences are similar to the jungle songs that Ramón used to sing. It might be the effect of the *toé*, but I soon feel myself in the low jungle: The humidity is the jungle air, and with my eyes closed I can hear a running stream, and her songs and the sounds of birds are indistinguishable.

Then she is blowing softly on the top of my head, I can smell her breath, redolent of coca and *llibta*. I hear her say, "Go with me," in Spanish—didn't Antonio say that she spoke no Spanish? Never mind. I let my body and mind go, my jaw goes slack and I lean my head back into her hands and I am soaring.

It was the briefest of sensations, so unexpected, that it startled me out of it. I opened my eyes and saw that the room was dark, the only light was the brassy reflected glow of the Primus. Antonio was sitting across from me, his chin on his chest, following the meditation, listening to her songs. But for that instant, I was flying over the jungle, over Ramón's hut, descending toward the lagoon, where I saw myself standing and staring into the water there below me.

—Another train stop—please, no. Antonio will want to get up and—false alarm—

Back with La Mascadora. She draws her hand down my face to close my eyes. She is still blowing on my head, slowly suspiring like a low steady whistle. I close my eyes again and see, feel, completely sense an oval divided down the middle, glowing blue-white, with a sort of golden nimbus or aura around it. It appears so clearly there, suspended in the utter darkness. Its light seems to come from within, like a small sun, and I am distinctly aware that I am *observing* it. She is still behind me, holding my head, and suddenly I have the inspiration that I am seeing my own head, my brain, even, from above, from her point of view.

Regardless, I hear her now, speaking to Antonio with the tone of approval. Even with my concentration broken I can see this glowing form, and as I incline my head forward, it moves as well. She takes her hands away and I open my eyes. Antonio is still sitting across from me, and La Mascadora is dipping a wooden bowl into a bucket of ice water. She moves behind me and pours it through the hole and down my steaming spine. "Inhale!" says Antonio, and I gasp—inhale a scream and I can barely keep from leaping up and destroying the clay oven as I submit to this torture four times—down my front and sides. Then I step out of the oven and she hands me an old, clean towel to wrap around my waist. There is a wool blanket on the cot and she tells me to lie there, to sleep. I close my eyes and see other eyes, animal eyes staring at me. I open my eyes as Antonio and the woman are leaving the room. I tell Antonio that there are eyes staring at me, and he tells me that the owl is the power animal of the *toé*. He tells me to rest.

It's wonderful in the wool blankets. My body is toned and glowing still with the heat of the sauna and the stimulation of the water, and I doze off, staring with my eyes closed back into the yellow-rimmed slit-eyes that are disembodied there before me.

I don't know how long I napped, but I am awakened by the woman, sitting beside me, her right hand on my forehead, her left on my pelvic bone. Her fingers exert a constant pressure as she brings her mouth close to my belly and blows into it with that soft whistle of hers. I feel it penetrate me—the oddest sensation—then she sings into my abdomen in that jungle-cadence tongue. One by one, at each of my chakras, a different song for each. I am filled with her breath and a joyful contentment. My stomach trouble has disappeared. She has removed the lid from the pressure cooker and filled the still steaming water with bottles from the counter. She withdraws one—a Coca Cola bottle filled with a semi-liquid white stuff. She pours a few drops onto my belly and massages it in with her fingers. Antonio tells me it is *cebo de tigre*—fat from the spotted jaguar. The other bottles are similarly filled with fat thinning in the hot water: *cebo de condor, de aguila real, de jaguar,* even a tiny clear vial of *cebo de boa*. Each in turn gets massaged into one of my chakras, *centros*.

I fell asleep again, and awoke to the smell of tobacco. I stood, unsteadily—something was wrong with me—and walked to the door into the living room.

They were sitting on the floor on opposite sides of her *mesa*—a large piece of some kind of plant fiber with woven geometric designs— spread out on the dirt floor. The four directions were marked out by long strings of colorful beads. There were eagle claws, a bird skull, a variety of stones and ceramic pieces, a few shells and small bottles, and each direction featured a pile of the most gloriously golden yellow corn kernels I had ever seen—they fairly glowed in the light of the dozen or so candles that flickered in every nook and cranny of the room.

And they were not alone. There in the room were other things that I saw and felt, suggestions of things vibrating in the thick vapor of tobacco smoke, but I could not stay—I never saw distinctly what they were—for in the next instant I was running through the kitchen and out the back door to a little garden, where I retched my guts out, evacuated my stomach and bowels.

The sounds of my distress brought Antonio to the door. He helped me back in and I splashed water on my face, and joined them at the *mesa*. The air had cleared somewhat. I had missed their private ceremony, but was able to watch La Mascadora close her circle without a word, using gestures only to salute the four directions and the Earth and sky. And I watched her apply her fats to Antonio's chakras and rub a sticky orange ointment into his joints—his ankles and knees and elbows and shoulders and wrists and fingers.

Then they shared the task of purifying me with smoke, took turns drawing deeply on a pipe that I knew was hers—I had seen it before, twelve years ago: long hardwood bowl carved in the likeness of an owl, stem and bit made from a length of antler—and blowing the smoke on my chakras front and back.

My physical symptoms were gone. I felt utterly at peace, joyfully refreshed, and I dozed off again, watching La Mascadora de la Coca purify Antonio with the smoke of her tobacco.

The next thing that I remember was Antonio waking me before dawn, saying that I must get dressed. We had to leave.

I closed the notebook on the pencil and stared out at the desolate *altiplano* passing us at fifty miles an hour. Antonio had fallen asleep but woke with a smile, his eyes on my journal. He would not ask, so I handed it to him. Twenty minutes later he handed it back to me and said: "I remember the first time I visited La Mascadora in her place in the mountains."

"This place exists, then?"

"Clearly."

"And you went there?"

"As you did," he replied, "although I was much younger. Your way of describing the sensation is wonderful—the sphere that reflects everything on its surface. It is an astonishing sensation and a true test of intent to maintain that state of being. For me, there was also a color, a sort of emerald greenness to my disembodied self. I thought it was the color of wisdom." He smiled fondly at the memory of it.

"I was confused. I had been dreaming. I was ill with a high fever, asleep in a cot in the back room of a church. I was dreaming of Condor Cancha—that is what the Incas called Machu Picchu. Of course, I did not know the place then—I had never been there—I was dreaming of a city in the clouds. But it was Condor Cancha that I was dreaming of, and in the dream I was tired and sought shelter, a place to sleep. So I found a place and fell asleep in my dream, and that is how I first entered the domain that is beyond dreaming. I saw my old friend in her little house in the snow. She welcomed me inside, and I was frightened by all that I saw and felt. When I saw the warmth of the candle flame, smelled its burning, and tasted its heat, I became disoriented. I remember that I tried to focus on a butterfly that was tacked to the dirt wall, but then—" he snapped his fingers, "I was back in my dream." He looked at me. "I was asleep in a corner of the city in the clouds, one of the ruined chambers of Condor Cancha—Machu Picchu. And I heard her voice calling to me to visit with her, to accept the change in my vision and to be still, to learn to be with her there." He turned away and stared through the dusty window pane. I watched his reflection. "And I let myself go back to her and I began to learn that the integrity of the dream body, that sphere of awareness, depended upon my intent. If I was there to learn and abandon all of my preconceptions, I could master the stillness of my dream body. I learned how to be conscious without being

162

self-conscious, and this was a very profound lesson; for it allowed me to go with her into the night, to witness and learn the skill of projecting my intent into an animal—what it is to be a jungle cat, to fly as a great bird of prey, to wander across the tundra among a herd of elk . . ."

"Elk?"

"And once a wolf," he nodded. "You see, we traveled together to far distant places. One of these was away to the north, Alaska, perhaps, who knows? This was a very long time ago, I have not done such things for many years."

He fell silent again and I wanted to encourage him, but I held my tongue and my breath. I was not used to such disclosure from this man. There was something disconcerting about it. His exposition of his philosophy, his science, his art, had never been personal.

"Sometimes she would come to me in my dreams, invite me to accompany her in that realm that is beyond the dream. It always happened when I was aware of myself dreaming. And there would come the brush of feathers, the glint of a round black eye, the flash of a hard yellow beak— she always came as a bird—and I would leave myself there dreaming and go with her. And whatever I had been dreaming was nothing compared to the experience of the dream space. The richness of it, the common sense that you described to me was intoxicating. But whenever I would feel the power of it, whenever I became aware of the wonder of it, whenever my thoughts or feelings strayed from the purpose—" he made a fist—"there I would be, back in my body, dreaming, unable to wake up."

"How old were you?"

"Fifteen or sixteen years old, I think."

"Who is this woman?"

He looked at me; pulled his head back sightly to see my whole face, for we were seated next to each other. "Yes, you see that she is something more than the healers and the *ayahuasceros* that you know so well." He turned slightly in his seat, to face me as best he could. "She is a shaman of the North," he said. "She has mastered the skills of the healer, and of the spirit warrior who conjures fear and conquers death—the work of the South and the West; she works beautifully with the energy body and knows the songs of the jungle, of the plants and the animals. And she has spent the past forty years of her life in mastering the lessons of the North. She is El Viejo's heir. She has freed herself from time. She has learned what it is to be invisible, and she has acknowledged the secret that is so sublime that we keep it even from ourselves."

"Three lessons?"

"Do not count them. A lifetime's work should not be reduced to formula."

I nodded hastily. "And you?" He raised his eyebrows at me. "You told me once—I wrote it down and have repeated it—that few complete the Medicine Wheel, that many who follow its . . . program are content to stop along the way—"

"Those who master the South become healers, often," he said. "The *ayahuasceros* are shamans of the West—"

"But there are few true 'persons of knowledge,' " I continued. "Your own work—"

He cut me off politely: "Yes, I have completed my work of the North. I know what La Mascadora knows, although she holds a place of distinction, of honor among my people, and a responsibility that I do not assume. The difference between us is our vision of the future and our place as teachers—our work of the East. She chose long ago to dedicate herself to our tradition, here, in the land of the Incas. She does, in fact, live much of the year in a small house in the mountains, in the snow, with a small group of apprentices—some have studied with her for fifty years. She serves her people—our people—in a traditional way." He held out his hand as though to offer me an example. "During the celebration of Corpus Christi, she descends from the *apu,* bearing with her a rock of ice from the sacred peak near her home. This is so that during the celebration of the Eucharist, of the body of Christ, the people may feed from the body of the sacred mountains. That is just one of the ways in which the traditions of our ancestors were assimilated into the traditions of our conquerors.

"She has given her life to maintaining the rituals and practices of the ancients. That is her choice, her vision of the East. But long ago I saw that the new shamans, the new caretakers of the Earth, would never rise from this place. They would come from the north. From your culture, from those who already rule the physical world. I have learned all that I have of philosophy and traditions far removed from those of my people, and found the truth in all of them and tried to teach that truth to my students, to those who were lucky enough to attend a university. I have divided my time and my task between the city and the country, between my responsibilities as a *profesor* and those of an Indian here. But I have never taught anyone as much as you have learned."

I thought about this for a long moment. About the inherent humility of his statement, the implicit compliment. Never before had I been so gripped by the importance of it all—what he knew and what it all could mean.

We arrived in Puno at seven P.M.

15

ONE HUNDRED TWENTY MILES SOUTHEAST OF Cuzco, the cultivated fields of the *altiplano* give way to a barren terra-cotta landscape 12,500 feet above sea level. The earth is the color of broken pottery and the sky is lapis lazuli, save where the unfiltered Sun burns white-hot. This is the land of *El Lago Sagrado,* the sacred lake, the sea at the top of the world—Titicaca, the highest navigable body of water on Earth. Popularly believed to be the source of the Amazon, the Lake Victoria of South America covers 3,200 square miles between Peru and Bolivia, and its "Mountains of the Moon" are called the Cordillera Real, the "Royal Range" of the Andes.

Once home to the most ancient cultures of the Americas, the Wari and Tiahuanaco tribes, which were assimilated by the Incas, the scorched soil has been inherited by the Aymara Indians, and the Uros have claimed the water. The Aymara cultivate the mineral-rich soil and grow the staple foods that their ancestors discovered and perfected: corn and potatoes, *quinoa* and *kiwicha* grains.

And the Uros cultivate the waters of the lake where the legends were born. There are fewer than one hundred families of these natives living on twenty or thirty manmade floating islands of reeds that drift on the surface of Lake Titicaca. From a shy, superstitious culture, they have harvested the lake grass to build their crescent-shaped boats and to keep themselves afloat for over a thousand years. Perhaps they have been the most susceptible to the overall sense of impermanence that looms in the atmosphere of this semi-mythical place. It is in evidence everywhere: in the islands decaying under the feet of the Uros, and in the makeshift city built by the Aymara at Puno, the harbor city on the Peruvian coast of Titicaca.

We arrived at rush hour; that is to say that the market was jammed with people, and the market is next to the train station. We stepped out into the throng and dodged the taxi *cholos*—the rickety, three-wheeled bicycle-drawn rickshaws that are the preferred mode of transportation in the city. It was dusk, and the shadows were uncommonly long, and there was a pleasant, warm orange cast to the place that belied the cold air. Antonio made a few purchases, and we each bought a poncho. And as the Sun slipped behind the Cordillera Real and the gas lamps were lighted in the market, Antonio hired a cab driver to take us to Sillustani.

The things that can be known but not told are not limited to abstract esoterica. I know what Sillustani did to me—how it made me feel, how being there in the night with Antonio is an experience that will always live in my memory as dreams live, and in my old age I will wonder whether or not I lived it or dreamed it—if, in my old age, I am still able to distinguish between the two. Of course, Antonio would disagree with my premise; he did, two days later. He told me that to a shaman, if a thing can be known, then it can be told, because the shaman's experience is the source of the story and the shaman is the one who tells it.

Fifteen miles from Puno, driving purposefully along a desolate dirt road, the skewed twin beams of the cab's headlights shining on nothing in particular, our driver leaned anxiously forward over the steering wheel. What he was looking for is a mystery to me—some landmark? a point-of-no-return sign? Whatever it was, he stopped the car finally, decisively, and said something to Antonio, sitting beside him in the passenger seat. He turned the key and the engine died.

"We have to walk," said my friend, and the taxi door creaked as he opened it. I got out and looked around.

We might have been on the surface of the moon; there was nothing but rock-strewn ground, a slight rise to the right. Antonio drew a deep breath of the crisp air and smiled at me. His face was a pallid mask in the moonlight. "He is unwilling to go any farther," he said. "He will wait for us." He looked to the left and indicated for me to follow, and off we went; the crunch of our boots was the only sound for miles around—I am sure of it—until the taxi's engine turned over once, twice, caught, and the gear engaged and we stopped to watch the red taillights disappear over the horizon.

We looked at each other and Antonio shrugged. "We will find him," he said, and turned, and continued on.

And then we crested the incline and I saw Sillustani for the first time.

As the curtain rises, the stage is in darkness. Slowly the lights come up to reveal the set. To see Sillustani in the silver shades between black and white, and to witness the alchemical change from silver to gold as the Sun rises, is to see something unforgettable. In this place where the days are white gold and the nights are polished silver, Sillustani is best approached in the night, in the moonlight.

We stood on a broad, flat promontory of a peninsula two hundred feet above the black mirror surface of a small lake, where the near-full moon was reflected in dazzling ripples of silver light. There in the middle of the lake, silhouetted against the sparkling moonlight, was an unnatural sight— an island, a truncated mountain rising out of the water, a mountain whose top had been lopped off with one swift stroke of an empyrean sickle—it is perfectly level, utterly flat. Yet it was not the sight of this geographical anomaly that caught my breath, but the things that loomed in my peripheral vision.

Round megalithic columns, colossal monuments made from mammoth blocks of perfectly cut and fitted granite. There are eight of them in the immediate vicinity. There is nothing to which they can be compared without contrivance; they are so simple, so massive and imposing. Inverted, broader at the top than at the base, thirty to forty feet high, they stand in uncontested possession of the brittle red soil from which they rise; they command the peninsula and dwarf anyone who stands in their presence.

They are not the disembodied monoliths of Easter Island staring sightlessly out to sea, but structures with a function, designed to serve a purpose. Did they contain something? If so, what? And why here?

"It is a cemetery," Antonio said.

I glanced at him, but my attention was jerked back to the *chullpas*—that is what the Aymara call them, *las chullpas de Sillustani*. If this was a cemetery, then these were tombs, and Sillustani must be a graveyard of kings or giants, rulers of the world itself, perhaps. . . .

We walked to a place near the center of the stage, instinctively avoiding the moon shadows cast by the towering reliquaries.

Antonio pointed to the left; his arm made a slow arc to the right, and I saw that they were everywhere. For as far as I could see in the night, the faraway landscape, uninhabited, desolate as a moonscape, was marked by similar towers of stone. There was nothing else. Nothing but brittle red soil, gray in the night, the sky bright with stars and the silver-white moon.

He nodded at the lake surrounding the flat-topped island. "This is Umayo," he said. "The word means 'head' or 'source.' And that is the island of the same name. It is marvelous to look at." He turned to face the towers that blotted out the stars. I noticed that some of them were partially ruined—huge granite blocks, four feet by four feet and weighing at least ten tons, had tumbled away and lay half-buried in the soil as though embedded there on impact. The hollow interiors of these half-toppled towers were exposed; some had been filled in with stones and rubble. "And these are the *chullpas,*" he said. "The tombs of the caretakers of the Earth. Sillustani is the burial ground of the ancient shamans of Peru."

July 7

Antonio has wandered off to collect firewood. I offered to help, but he wanted to do it himself. Over the edge of the cliff there are bushes and scattered tufts of grass.

Sitting on a rock on the edge of the cliff, looking back on the *chull-pas,* the steady chirp of a cricket somewhere enhances, almost amplifies the acute silence that reigns here. It is light enough to write by. I want to capture an impression . . .

Time has stopped here. It hangs, suspended in the air. You can almost see it shimmering, the air crackling with something like static electricity. It is palpable, the atmosphere of this place, and it can distract you. My attention is constantly drawn away from where I am looking. Like a dog that sees things where there is nothing to see—I look left, suddenly, nothing. What was that? Nothing but something invisible, something pendant.

I asked Antonio what we were doing here. And he has told me that we are here to finish the work that I began when I came back to Peru.

"This is the place of the North," he said. I watched him construct his little four-sided framework of sticks and dry grass. He was on his knees, intent upon his work. His *mesa* was still wrapped, leaning against a block of granite to his right. "Where the bodies of our ancestors were laid to rest and the ancient memories are honored. They were the masters of the Four Winds, and I pray that all of the work that you have done has prepared you to learn the elements of their mastery. That is one of the reasons to be here. Only those who have already died may come here with the purpose that we carry." He reached into the folds of his two ponchos and withdrew a small flat piece of wood that looked like driftwood, and a straight stick ten inches long. These he set side by side next to the tiny pyre of twigs and grass, then rocked back onto his haunches with a grunt.

I have never been very comfortable in cemeteries, and Antonio's warning—for that is how I interpreted it—sounded altogether ominous. Prepare yourself now, if you are unfortunate enough to have come here before your time. I had wrongly assumed that I was here as his companion, a passive witness to his work, an innocent bystander. I should have known better. I had no wish for another worse-than-death experience. The image of the *pischaco,* the "dispirited one" of Sacsayhuaman, had not completely rotted from my memory. My night of despair in the jungle still haunted me.

But I *was* prepared, I decided, and instantly realized that my resolution was more a choice than an evaluation of readiness.

"Is there another reason to be here?" I asked, surprised at the effect of my voice in the silence that was absolute but for the cricket; it was as though I could talk to myself and still be heard.

"Perhaps," he said. "And perhaps we will discover it tomorrow or the next day." I shivered involuntarily and drew my poncho closer. I wondered when he was planning to light the fire. But Antonio was always methodical—he would light the fire when it was appropriate; now he simply leaned forward and clasped his hands.

"The Incas who built these tombs," he said, "were a practical people who assimilated all who were here before them. There were the Wari and the Tiahuanacos who came from here." He lifted his chin and swept the landscape with his eyes. "And there were others, remote and primitive and likely to remain so. To unite these diverse peoples—all of the tribes from the lowland jungles to the highest mountains to the shores of the sea—to form an empire, the Incas forged a new mythology—a myth of origin that would identify their Eden, pinpoint the place as if a map were given. . . . Those who mustered the courage were then able to return there for certain purpose—"

He stopped and cocked his head to listen. It took me a moment to realize what he heard: the silence that was suddenly complete—the cricket had stopped. He looked at me and raised his eyebrows and smiled mischievously. His face was utterly joyful, and for an instant I glimpsed Antonio Morales as a young man of the 1940s. It happened in an instant when his cheeks lifted with the smile and his eyes caught the moonlight. There was something chilling about it. Every other time that I had been in ceremony with this man, I was the student participant and he was the master, and there was a confident gleam in his eyes on which I had come to depend. Tonight the joy in those eyes unnerved me: I realized that *he* was the participant, and no one was in charge.

Now, as though the cricket's stillness was a cue, he bent to the task of lighting the fire. He pulled a wad of fleecy material from his pocket and pulled at it and fluffed it and set it next to the flat piece of wood and set the end of the straight stick into a dimple in the wood and began to rub it between his palms with such speed and dexterity that his hands were a blur.

And in place of the cricket was the squeak-squeak of wood against wood. I could hardly believe it—we had always used matches.

The little stick twirled and squeaked for a full five minutes, and Antonio picked up where he had left off.

"In all of the countries north of the equator—and remember that the great cultures of history developed north of the equator—God is a descending god. Think of the Greeks, the Romans, the Christians, the Muslims. The Divine comes from the heavens and descends to the Earth." He leaned closer to inspect the wad of flax. "But for the Incas—the only great culture to develop south of the equator—the god-force is ascending. It rises from the Mother Earth." His eyes followed a delicate ribbon of smoke up from the tip of the stick and the dimple in the wood. Faster and faster still he twirled the stick between his palms. He leaned in and breathed on the flax wad.

"It rises from the Earth to the heavens like the golden corn." He stopped and the stick fell away, and he took the flax between his thumb and forefinger and leaned over it and breathed. A couple of orange sparks fell to the ground and I saw another orange speck worming its way through the fibers, igniting others, glowing brighter as he breathed, and then the orange was yellow and there was a flame and he placed the wad in the center of the dry grass. He sat back on his haunches and watched the flames catch and crackle and lick the air. "From the Earth to the heavens," he said, and grinned at me. And while the fire spread and he fed it with twigs and sticks and lengths of gnarled branches, he went on.

"And those who are buried here at Sillustani are the men and women who spent their lives acquiring knowledge, germinating and cross-germinating their wisdom and their corn, discovering and understanding the forces of Nature and the relationship between the Sun and the Earth and the Moon and the stars. They practiced a way of knowing that is . . . an alchemy of life. The alchemy of your European ancestors consisted of taking dead matter—base elements such as sulfur and lead—and placing it in a crucible and applying fire in a vain effort to make gold. But my people used living matter, placed it in the crucible of the Earth, under the fire of the Sun, and produced corn, a living gold." He brought his hands together and leaned over them, nearer the fire. "The farmers perfected the alchemy with the soil, and the shamans practiced the alchemy of the soul—not to produce *aurum vulgaris,* the common gold, but *aurum philosophus.*" He leaned back, away from the fire, and his face darkened. "The shaman does not do this alone. He or she must call on the future to bear witness to this final act of power. This is why I have asked you to come along with me." His face was in the fire again. "When the old ones who are buried here achieved mastery, when they knew what it was to be invisible, when they could influence the *past* as well as the future, and when they were able to keep a secret even from themselves, then the secret was revealed to them."

The fire was burning freely now, revealing the colors that were within its hemisphere of light: the russet soil, the red and brown of Antonio's poncho, his mahogany features, his gray hair. "You are not making this journey merely to comfort an old man," he said, and his eyes sparkled with firelight. "You returned to Peru because you and I are linked together by our work and our knowledge and our passion for the human mind. I wanted you to come back as you have—alone and looking for what you have yet to learn. And you have made another circuit of the Medicine Wheel. You confronted your past and all of the expectations that you had accumulated, and you shed it along the road to Machu Picchu. You faced death again in the jungle and more acutely, for it was not your death only that poisoned you with fear. And all this while, the knowledge has been whispering to you. You have tasted invisibility in the dream state. You were correct, that a perfect sphere reflects everything in the universe—everything but *itself,* my friend, everything but you." He gave me a moment to think about this, then: "You were invisible when you inhabited the condor. You know this sensation now; and as you learn to gather your intent and master the stillness of that dream body, you will be able to know greater things." He waved his hand as though to dismiss the subject. "There is more to invisibility than this clever example, but you should know that it is one of the fundamental concepts of mastery—it has been used to acquire knowledge and to impart it to others for a thousand years." He placed another bough on the fire.

"Time," he said. He closed his eyes and breathed deeply. "The ancient ones here knew that there was a relationship between time and light. That light has no time. Nothing can travel at the speed of light but light itself. If we approach the speed of light, we must become light. When we become light—an *Inca,* a Child of the Sun—then time is dissolved." He lifted another small branch of deadwood. "We all know that our deeds today affect tomorrow, that our smallest gestures influence destiny, that the future of our species changes constantly with every action of every living thing on Earth." He snapped the branch in half and seemed to consider which half to give to the fire before tossing them in together. "But can you imagine that today's experience might also depend on something that happens tomorrow? That you and I might not be sitting here were it not for something that happens a month from now? The second lesson of mastery is that time is polychronic *and* monochronic—it does not fly like an arrow only. It also turns. Like a wheel." He traced a circle in the air with his fingertip. "When these two kinds of time intersect, that is sacred time, ritual time, when you can influence the past and summon destiny from the future."

He paused and looked away from the fire, over his shoulder, then up into the sky so full of stars that it was the blackness in between them that invited our gaze—was it a black sky filled with stars, or a shining sky dappled black?

"And the secret?" I asked as he lowered his eyes to meet mine across the fire.

"The secret follows from mastery of invisibility and of time. It is not the secret that is important; it is our ability to keep this secret, it is how we hold it. Knowing it is like knowing the future, and who but those who understand that time turns like a wheel can manage to know the future and not let it upset their balance? If your faith in reality is based on a belief that time moves in one direction only, then the foundation of your faith will be shattered by an experience of the future. This does not concern the shaman, because the shaman has no need for faith—the shaman has experience. Nevertheless, it takes great skill to know the future and not allow your knowledge to spoil your actions or your intent.

"Those who are buried here knew such things. They slipped through time, tasted our destiny. They understood the importance of life on Earth.

"That is why they worshiped the Sun and the Earth. They knew that there would be no life on Earth if it were not for the Sun, that life is the direct result of their union. They knew this before there were scientific formulas explaining photosynthesis or equating energy and mass and the speed of light. They were practical in this. The Sun is the father and the Earth is the mother and *their* parents were *one* —Illa Tici Viracocha—neither male nor female, energy in its purest form. They honored their mother and father by making *ayni*. This is the basis of all Andean shamanism. It is a principle of reciprocity. You make *ayni* to the Pachamama, the Mother Earth, and she is pleased and returns your gift with fertility and abundance. You make *ayni* to the Sun, and he returns your gift with warmth and light. The *apus,* the great mountain peaks, give you strength to endure your work; the heavens give you harmony. Make *ayni* to all people and they will honor you in return. It is a beautiful principle.

"They say that the shaman lives in perfect *ayni*—the universe reciprocates his every action, mirrors his intent back to him as he is a mirror to others. And that is why the shaman lives in synchronicity with Nature. The shaman's world mirrors the shaman's will and intent and actions.

"We begin by making *ayni* out of primitive superstition—to 'please the gods.' Later, we make *ayni* out of habit, as part of a ceremony. These forms of *ayni* are performed out of fear or convention, not out of love. *Eventually* we make *ayni* because we *must,* because we feel it here—" he touched his breast. "They say that only then is *ayni* perfect, but I believe that *ayni* is always perfect, that our world is always a true reflection of our intent and our love and our actions. That is my opinion, but I think that it is a good one. The condition of our world depends upon the condition of our consciousness, of our souls."

The fire had burned down considerably. One by one, he placed the remaining sticks and twists of wood into the flames. Then he unbound his *mesa* and rolled out the woven square of Inca cloth and placed his few objects in their proper places.

As I watched him I thought: Why now? Why had he waited so long to tell me all of this? That was when the suspicion first entered my mind. I let it in, but refused to look at it; instead I contented myself with the fact that although his words would have fascinated me in a classroom or on a hill in the middle of the *altiplano,* here, in Sillustani, among the *chullpas,* they had the effect of a revelation. A testament of sorts.

"Tonight," he resumed, when I had finished my last thought, "we will make *ayni* to the ancestors, the storytellers, the caretakers of the Earth, those who have sown and cultivated divine consciousness across time. They lived in the mountains and in the jungles and they left this world alive—they died knowing that their children would speak for them, that they would speak through their children.

"We honor them with respect and thanksgiving, for it is on their shoulders that we stand tonight and tomorrow and the night that will follow. It is their wisdom and experience that we seek. There will be a sign if we are to proceed with our journey. Have no doubts. Simply close your eyes and allow those whose bodies rest here to speak to you."

But I watched him instead. I watched him stand by the fire, his features glowing in the low-angle firelight, a reverse silhouette against the sparkling black sky. He stood there with his head bowed for a long time, so long that he appeared almost to sleep on his feet. But his back was straight, his poise a study in concentration and . . . humility.

Then he raised his head and opened his eyes. He spoke steadily, intimately, just above a whisper.

"To the winds of the South, Amaru, great serpent—ancient ones, gentle healers of the past. I call on you. You who were the first to offer us the fruit of the tree of knowledge . . . wrap your coils of light around us. Know that we have shed our past as you shed your skin. Waters that run deep in the Earth, cleanse us and purify us, for we come with honor and respect—in the ancient way."

He slipped his hand into the folds of his poncho and withdrew a handful of something that he placed on the ground on the southern side of the *mesa*—a tiny pile of bright golden kernels of corn and fresh green whole leaves of coca. Then he turned to the west; his back was to me.

"To the winds of the West, mother-sister jaguar, bridge between the worlds, ancestral stewards of life—the twice-dead and twice-born. We salute you with our hearts and our simple gifts, and invite you to sit here tonight in our medicine circle. Know that we, too, are twice-born. We have already died. We leave no tracks, and death may no longer claim us."

He placed another offering on the soil and turned to face north. There was a new note in his voice.

"To the winds of the North, the many-faced dragon, grandmothers and grandfathers—you who wove the spiral threads of time into a cloak of mystery that you may move invisibly. . . . We come with love and gratitude and ask that you welcome us. Bless us in our work and sit in council with us tonight. Let us look into your eyes. Feast with us across time, and know that those yet to be born will one day stand on our shoulders as we have stood on yours."

Again the tiny mound of corn and the coca leaves. When he turned to the east, I saw that his cheeks were wet, his eyes were glistening. He blinked once, twice; a tear broke free and fell from his cheek to the hard red soil. Perfect *ayni*.

"To the winds of the East, Aguila Real, great eagle who soars from the *apus* to the Sun and back, great seers and visionaries, mythmakers and storytellers, we are here to see you and to celebrate your vision. Fly high above us tonight that we may learn to soar to the great heights that you once mastered and that we dream of. Guide us and protect us that we may always fly wing to wing with the Great Spirit."

There was a tear stuck on the end of his moustache as he bent over to make the offering to the East. Then he took up a silver-capped antique glass flask from his *mesa*—the flask that always held his medicine of ritual and vision, the muddy green preparation of San Pedro cactus and cleansing herbs.

"To Father Sun, and Mother Earth—" he unscrewed the cap and emptied the flask into the ground—all of it. "And the Great Spirit, Viracocha, know that all that we do is in your name."

Then he replaced the cap and set aside the flask and sat across from me on the west side of the *mesa*. I stared at him, at his emotion. And he withdrew a folded handkerchief from under his ponchos and wiped his high cheeks; I am sure that his hand was trembling, and again, the suspicion caught my breath . . .

"Close your eyes, my friend. There is a variety of time that is synchronous with Nature. That is sacred time—when *ayni* is made and reciprocated, when pure intent is mirrored back to us, when our actions are sanctified. We have asked for permission to continue what we have begun. Close your eyes and let the ancestors speak to you."

But they were his words that I heard. The fire had died to a few glowing embers cushioned in white ash and my body was shivering, my mind spinning with all that he had said, all that he had inferred.

I do not know how long I sat there on the hard earth, listening to Antonio's narrative and invocation echoing in my head. It could have been five minutes or fifteen. Could I ever capture his meaning? What was so clearly stated and with such passion—could I remember it all? Could I believe it?

And then there was a sound, a high-pitched fluttering, low to the ground—a small bird like a sparrow flying fast in a wide circle around us. I could hear the flurry of its little wings flapping near . . . far . . . near, around and around it went, and then:

I open my eyes to look and she stands there behind him; I see her standing behind Antonio's shoulder. The little bird continues to circle us, but I never see it; I am staring back at Antonio's old friend, the Q'ero shamaness, La Mascadora de la Coca, there, behind him. His eyes are closed in meditation, but hers are fixed on mine. As I look, she turns her head, up toward the *chullpa* to my left and her right. Reluctantly I follow her bright eyes, look up to see the horrible thing squatting on its upper edge—a condor, that *vultur gryphus* of the Andes, man-sized, hunched over, its wings folded, its wrinkled face hanging down between its . . . shoulders. It looks like a deformed man, a hunchback with a feather shroud. It shifts its weight awkwardly, then shudders, its feathers all ruffled—

She smiles at me, La Mascadora, and this is an invitation to fly. I can project my will into this thing that she has brought here; I can perform the lesson that she taught me, and fly to the Amazon now.

But I won't. Antonio's face, passive and serene in the firelight, reminds me of my choice, my preparation. So I smile back at her and nod and close my eyes and know instantly that she is with Antonio, loving him like a sister, testing *me* to know that he travels with a reliable friend, a true *compadre* . . .

"Compadre . . ." whispers Antonio.

And I opened my eyes on his, shining at me from across the *mesa*, and there was no sign of the woman—in fact, I had not opened my eyes until he called to me. A chill passed through me. He raised his eyebrows in a question. I nodded to him that all was well. He smiled, held my eyes with his, and drew them up, skyward; together we raised our eyes to the heavens.

The stars were falling over Sillustani. Bright white pinpoints of light tracing arcs that crisscrossed the night sky, flaming white, bursting, raining down through the silence. I held my breath; I was spellbound.

"Ah . . ." Antonio's uninhibited sigh.

I glanced at him, his face was upturned as though to catch the drops of pure white light that seemed to shower the little lake and the peninsula and the silent tombs of his ancestors. Antonio Morales looked to the heavens, and the heavens reflected his ecstasy with perfect *ayni*.

16

Over the Mountains of the Moon
Down the Valley of the Shadow
Ride boldly, ride, the Shade replied
If you search for El Dorado.

—*Edgar Allan Poe*

IT WAS THREE O'CLOCK IN THE MORNING WHEN
we found our taxi and our driver—asleep in the back seat—nearly a mile
from the *península encantada*.

We checked into a hotel in Puno and slept for eight hours, then
stepped out into the dazzling light of midday at Titicaca, where the Sun's
light is so pure and of such intensity that it reflects from every surface and
you squint against the glare, and objects that should be defined in the light
are hazy and vague.

The lake stretched before us like a forgotten sea. One hundred twenty
miles long, thirty-seven miles at its widest, the lake has been sounded to over
nine hundred feet, although natives claim that (*dicen que*) the sacred lake is
bottomless.

Even in the streets of Puno you can feel the something in the air that
sharpens your senses, keeps you alert, almost restless. This widely reported
sense is commonly attributed to the 12,000-foot altitude, but there is more
to it: something friable, something like tension.

We ate a lunch of lake trout and yellow rice and grilled potato at a
street vendor's stand on the long concrete jetty where the fishing boats

and the cargo ship that crosses from Puno to La Paz are moored. The latter looks like a derelict, a lost and lonely vessel abandoned by its squadron, purchased from some country's merchant marine fleet in the 1940s, dismantled and hauled into the Andes 12,000 feet above the surface of the sea.

Antonio was anxious to get to Copacabana, so we caught a bus at shortly after one P.M. and bounced along the rutted dirt road that runs along the marshlands of the Peruvian coast. Twenty miles from Puno there is a police checkpoint, and a uniformed young man with a machine gun slung over his shoulder climbed aboard and asked to see our papers, and I realized that I had left my passport in Cuzco. It had not occurred to me that we would be leaving the country. This was trouble. I pretended to be traveling alone so as not to involve Antonio. I told the officer that I was an American doctor, that I was going to Juli, twenty-five miles this side of the Bolivian border. He gave me the eye, but I got away with it. We were still two hours from Yunguyo, the Peruvian border town, and suddenly our whole enterprise was in jeopardy.

But the bus driver, who had overheard my explanation, assured me that he had a friend at the crossing station. Did I have fifty dollars? Well, sure.

Unfortunately his friend was away for the day, and I negotiated my passage with a sullen border guard who looked like Ernie Kovacs in starched khakis and aviator sunglasses and brilliantined hair. Eighty-five dollars bought me a *salvoconducto*—safe passage documents. Fifty yards down the road, the Peruvian's Bolivian counterpart examined my papers front and back and assessed me another fifty dollars for forty-eight hours in his country.

Getting back into Peru was going to be dicey.

We arrived in Copacabana in the late afternoon. There is something desolate and bone-white about the town that has forever occupied this little headland that points to the Island of the Sun.

The Copacabana Peninsula is one of the most ancient sites in the Americas, the way station on the pilgrimage to the all-but-forgotten Mecca of the Western hemisphere. Beneath the terra-cotta soil are other cities suspended in strata of rock and clay, enigmatic cultures that predate even the ancient Tiahuanacos, who were assimilated by the Incas. Copacabana is a sacred place, a threshold to mystery, like El Medina is to Mecca. It is not the city itself that is important, however, but the space that it occupies, the function it serves; and there is a feeling of impermanence to the concrete and adobe buildings, as though they were built with the certain knowledge that they would one day be buried. So the homes and municipal facilities are functional but not aesthetic; the buildings are angular, the windows are square, and the walls have been crumbling forever. It is a city that knows its own mortality, understands its perpetual evanescence. There is something eerie about it, something self-conscious.

We walked up a steep cobbled street to the *zocalo*, the town square before the cathedral, the Basilica de Copacabana, past bleached pastel-painted homes and open doorways that are shops selling hats and nuts and candies and flour and corn and wine and beer and soda.

Baking in the direct and reflected rays of the fierce white heat of the Sun, the cathedral stands in bleak and impudent defiance of the tranquil resignation of this place. It is an outpost of Catholicism on a barren beachhead a stone's throw from the birthplace of pre-Columbian paganism. Inside, as though to overcompensate for its situation, the altar is a gold-leafed delirium of styles, a confusion of classical and baroque and incongruous primitive motifs. Its opulence is out of place: a dizzying spectacle that distracts the eye with indulgent detail. The marriage of Christian and pagan symbology and practice in Copacabana, Bolivia, is ripe for analysis by anthropologists, sociologists, ethnologists. There is something desperate about this far-flung sanctuary of Catholicism in a place founded by a people who looked to the Sun and the Earth for inspiration.

The basilica stands on the site of an Inca or Tiahuanaco shrine. Antonio and I descended to the cold catacombs beneath the altar of the *Virgen de Copacabana,* where rows of beeswax candles illuminate the black sweating stones, and we lit a candle for my father.

We ate supper in the restaurant bar of the hotel, then wandered down the street to the beach, because Antonio was anxious to watch the Sun set.

To the right the bay curves to the long stone jetty or seawall where the fishing boats—thirty-foot launches painted bright red or blue—are tied or beached. To the left the curve leads to a sparse grove of eucalyptus trees at the base of a volcano-shaped hill of red baked earth and irregular terraces. The shore itself is mostly stone, round stones, skipping stones, smooth and striated, spread evenly over hard-packed sand.

Before us the lake stretched to the horizon, broken here and there by odd islands, and to the right, four miles from the tip of the peninsula, the Island of the Sun. There was a breeze that moved the thin air and made spectral cat's paws on the dark gray surface of the lake, which had begun to reflect the fire in the sky. Like a sunset at sea, the whole skyline was burning and the waters were sparkling orange. And we could not take our eyes from the water and the sky and the line where they met, because we would miss something, some liquid moment of the transformation from day to night that here seems so alien, like sunset on a planet that orbits in the imagination of a science fiction writer. Verne or Poe or H. G. Wells might have created this landscape, this soundless sea and Sun-baked soil, where the air shimmers and the sky is painted in primary colors: red, yellow, green, and blue.

Then and there I realized the totality and inevitability of our journey together. This was not an exploration of consciousness to palliate my professional curiosity or existential angst. I was wittingly being drawn into someone else's drama, assuming a role that I was not sure that I could live up to—or wanted to. My father's death, although difficult, was expected—even welcome as a relief from his failed body and for the intimacy that we shared. My father had attended my birth, and I had attended his death. Antonio's parting—if indeed that is what he had planned—no matter what mystical explanation or excuse he offered, was a burden that I was unwilling to shoulder. It would take a better man than I to witness his self-immolation, because I was unwilling to let him go.

I was about to say something when the Sun dipped into the horizon and melted my resolve.

Like bold, broad brushstrokes on a painter's canvas, the sky read left to right, red, yellow, green, and blue—not blended like the colors of a rainbow, but distinct bands of color, one after the other.

It was then that my fancy defined what it was about the air. I realized that it was humming, vibrating at a frequency that, if we could hear it, would sound like the steady reverberation of a crescendo that has lingered here, echoing *in saecula saeculorum*, until the end of time.

We stayed on the beach for an hour and watched the phenomenon in the sky resolve itself into night, and my apprehension was transformed into a determination to serve whatever experience Antonio was crafting for me. I would not dissuade him from his purpose, no matter what it might mean to me. I had enough cash in my pocket to get me—and his body, if need be—back to Peru and to his people.

So we watched the Sun set and the night fall. Then we picked our way across the stones to the seawall, where Antonio made arrangements for our predawn trip to the Island of the Sun. We climbed the cobblestone street to our hotel and marched off to our rooms. I set my watch to wake me at half-past two, and stripped the other bed and covered myself, fully clothed, with all the sheets and blankets. I was asleep within minutes and awake seconds later. The high-pitched beeping of my wristwatch alarm in the chilly, blank darkness of my room was like a warning signal before a detonation. I sat up with a sense of panic, fumbled it off, and took a deep breath of cold air that startled my lungs.

There was a knock on the door. Antonio stood at the threshold, looking fresh and full of life. He gave me a bottle of spring water and a handful of toasted *kiwicha* seeds.

It was three o'clock in the morning and the lake was glassy, cleaved by the bow of our launch, and I sat wrapped in a gray wool poncho supplied by the skipper. I felt the cold air burn my face, and imagined what we looked like from above, where the burbling moan of our outboard would be a high-pitched whine echoing off the surface of the water, and our bow wave would be a long, narrow V pointing toward the Island of the Sun.

I barely remembered stumbling stiffly from the hotel to the jetty in the darkness, but the air and the water and that little-boy's sense of pre-dawn adventure had worked like a tonic and I was wide awake now, listening happily to Antonio explaining to the skipper the virtues of toasted *kiwicha* seeds.

I turned and folded my hands on the gunwale and rested my chin on my hands and felt the vibration of the motor and listened to the splish-splash of our bow wave and stared into the inky blackness of the bottomless lake. Then Antonio was by my side.

"Can we go any faster?" I asked.

"He refuses," said Antonio. "He will run his engine only at one-third throttle. He is afraid to wear it out." He grinned at the skipper's economy. "He is uneasy about this trip. I should have thought to find an Aymara native of the Island of Sun. They are not afraid to be on the water or the island in the night." He indicated the skipper with his eyes. "He is Aymara, but from the mainland, and superstitious. But it will be dawn soon, and all will be well."

An hour later we were within twenty yards of the shore, listening to the sound of our motor echoing from the steep rock escarpment of the southeast point of the island.

We landed in a cove and tied up to a stone jetty that bisects the little bay. We tied up only long enough to disembark. Antonio whispered something to the captain of the vessel, and we walked up the narrow pier to a grove of trees, maybe eucalyptus, then wandered to the right along the narrow shoreline.

It was still cold, bone-chilling, no longer a dry cold, because there on the rocky shore the breeze carried an invisible mist from the surface of this sea at the top of the world. The beach was narrow; a steep slope of scrub and diagonal layers of stratified rock rose behind us, and Antonio scaled this up twenty feet or so to gather wood. There were two hours until sunrise. From the look of the hill, he would not find much more than kindling and grass, so I went back to the bay; and at the foot of a magnificent stairway of stone disappearing up into the pitch black tangle of a pine and oak forest, I filled my arms with wood. Antonio had already fashioned a circle of stones around a tiny square scaffolding of kindling and grass. This time he sparked a match and touched it to the grass, and together we fashioned a sort of pyramid out of the log scraps and branches. And he asked me for the owl, the gold owl in my pocket.

I remember distinctly the sounds of that morning: the liquid sound of lake water lapping at the stony shore and the hissing snap of the fire; and the familiar low tone and cadence of Antonio's accent, reciting a familiar formula that grabbed me by the throat and held me spellbound. I watched his face, stared now and then at the tiny icon in his hand, while his words rose effortlessly through the thin precious air, carried aloft by the warm air of our fire.

"*El oro,*" he began without prompting, "the gold was made by the Sun's burning tear as it flowed down to the center of the Earth and cooled in the crevices of the rocks, in the valleys, by the streams that run to the heart of the Earth. And soon after the Earth erupted with life, the Children of the Sun emerged from the waters of the Earth's womb, here, in this place." His eyes were on the fire, and the fire danced in his eyes. Neither of us looked up, looked to the night-black lake, the waters that had always caressed this shore—the very waters of the story. It was as though I was hearing Genesis read to me in the shade of the tree of knowledge that grew in the center of Eden. Never before or since have I heard a story told in a more perfect setting, told at its source; but I kept my eyes on Antonio, and Antonio's attention was on the fire, on me, on the little owl in the palm of his hand.

"And like a newborn infant who knows where to find his mother's breast," he continued, "the Children of the Sun were born with the knowledge of their origins." He nodded. "That is why this is the first story ever told. It is the first thing known. We tell this story around a fire, because whenever we build a fire, we celebrate life by remembering the time when the Sun shed a tear of joy that landed on the Earth.

"So the Children of the Sun recognized the gold on the ground for what it was, even understood the ancient alchemy that created it in the crucible in the center of the Earth. And they celebrated and practiced this alchemy by using the fire of the Sun and the living soil of the Earth to create another gold, a living gold. And this was corn. Corn grew from the Earth and held the Sun in its center and nourished the Children of the Earth and the Sun and was valued above all other things. The growing of corn was a recreation of the alchemy of the Sun and the Earth, an alchemy that all their children could practice.

"And the gold that was on the ground and in the Earth was gathered by the Children of the Sun and worn close to their hearts and used to decorate their places of worship.

"But those who were born in the lowlands far from the Sun forgot their parents and believed that they were the children of man. They coveted the gold that was scarce in their own land, for among its properties was its magical ability to capture and hold the light of a candle or of the Sun and glow as though it were lit from within. And they came to this Eden, the land of the Children of the Sun, and found the gold that was in abundance and claimed this land and its gold in the name of the man they called their father.

"And they killed for it. And the blood of the Children of the Sun flowed over the gold that they wore over their hearts. So the Children of the Sun, the Incas, fled from the wrath of these men who did not know the Sun as their father. And they let it be known that they had gone to Vilcabamba, to a city of gold, the source of the thing that these other men killed for.

"This was true," he said. "They went to Vilcabamba."

He turned the gold owl slowly in the light of the fire; held it between his thumb and forefinger and turned it back and forth. "El Dorado," he whispered. Then he looked at the edge of the shore and up to the side of the hill and back to the object in his hand, as though he were considering the true source of the light. But it was hard to tell, because the Sun was rising.

"And the others, those who measured their riches in gold . . . mad for the gold, tried to follow, to pursue them, and many died trying to find Vilcabamba, El Dorado. But, you see, they were fooled. They were looking for a place, a place deep within the valleys of the great *apus*. But Vilcabamba is not a place. It is *Vilcabamba*, the Sacred Plain.

"The Incas fled to the Sacred Plain, those who could, for many were wise and knew the way. They left their bodies behind them, and their bodies were tortured and their hearts were ripped from their chests, but they had already left this world alive; they had gone to Vilcabamba."

That was when the Sun burst over the horizon, crested Illimani, the highest peak of the Cordillera Real, snowbound, glacial, 8,000 feet above the surface of the lake, now perfectly still in anticipation of the dawn.

"So the ruined city in the jungle at Espiritu Pampa—"

"Is just a place," he said. "You see, my old friend, we are truly Children of the Sun. The journey East is not just the return to one's home—one's community—to realize the visions and exercise the skills acquired along the Journey of the Four Winds. It is literally the return home—to the place whence we came—the source of life and the creative principle. It is the journey to Vilcabamba, the Sacred Plain. Not a place that man can walk to . . ."

"So," I said, as we climbed the 137 steps through the forest of eucalyptus and pine and mossy stone, "the Incas went to a place where the Spanish could not follow. A place they would never find."

"Because they did not know how to walk, and they did not know how to see the spaces in between things." Antonio grinned. "It is the very best version of the legend of the Children of the Sun and the fabled city of gold, don't you think?"

Yes, it was. But I could not help but wonder if the first story ever told was to be the last I heard from his lips.

According to legend the *pakarina*, the "hole whence life pours," set into the granite wall at the top of the steps on the Island of the Sun, is the source of Lake Titicaca. There are three algae- and moss-ringed spouts carved into the stone, through which the water has flowed steadily for over a thousand years—water coveted throughout South America for its healing properties. Here natives came once in their lives, paddling their reed boats or rafts to the island to drink from the first source, the first water, the spring that fed their Eden.

The outermost spouts represent polarity, male and female, the separation of the single source into two—so Antonio makes a *pago,* an offering of corn and coca and a splash of *pisco*, then steps into the narrow pool at the base of the fountain and places his hands under the spouts and brings them together to his forehead, his throat, his heart, his belly, then drinks the water from each of the spouts.

I follow his example and the icy water startles me. We fill our water bottles and begin to climb.

The Island of the Sun is a curious place of rock and brittle soil—not the red soil of Sillustani, but rose-tinted, sand-colored, like pink gold. Here and there are odd outcroppings of granite and igneous rock, evidence of volcanic activity. The ground is strewn with bits of stone with perfect hemispheres scooped out of them, as though bubbles had been trapped inside of them—air fossils . . .

And the higher we climb, the more I notice tiny shards of pottery, evidence of pre-Columbian earthenware bowls and urns and figures shattered and ground into the soil. I stoop to collect and examine various pieces; some are very old, some new. Antonio explains that natives from every corner of the continent have made pilgrimages to this place. For 5,000 years they have come to make their *pagos* at the birthplace of the Children of the Sun.

"Returning to the place of the birth of your people is a way of completing the wheel," he says. "It is the most appropriate place to make *ayni* in the Western Hemisphere."

I comment that such a pilgrimage is impossible for the Westerner, whose myth of origin begins with the exile from the Garden. What better way to lead a people than to take away their birthright and hold the Divine at arm's length and say, Follow me?

"But," says Antonio, "the Judeo-Christian tradition has served to unite a culture for 2,000 years. It is true that the arrogance of your people has caused much suffering and destruction. What is most difficult to understand is the hypocrisy of the faith, the breaking of commandments in the name of God."

The climb is steep and the Sun beats steadily on us. We shed our clothes as we go, and I notice for the first time Antonio's years. He is slow and methodical, picking his way carefully around craggy obstructions, climbing gingerly over steep, stratified rock formations jutting up through the crusty soil.

It is midday when we crest the top of the island. Antonio has fallen silent—not a word for the last two hours. He seems distracted now as he points ahead to a rock formation five hundred yards away. Our destination, he says. But we stop here and look around us. To the right the island slopes down to a grassy plain, where there is a small farm—there are quite a few Aymara families living here, farming the land, harvesting *quinoa, kiwicha,* potatoes, beans, and brilliant corn. And there are llamas for wool, fertilizer, meat; even their sinews are used for braided cording. Just offshore are two islands: one is wooded, pine trees growing evenly across its flat top, and another is utterly barren. And in the distance, five or six miles to the east, an island that looks for all the world like a gigantic boulder floating on the lake's surface. To the left there are terraces, wide, uneven steps of green crops planted in neat rows. And there is a little bay—I can only see a fraction of it: a sandy beach, a sunken stone jetty . . .

I estimate that we have climbed five hundred feet. We began at lake level, so we must be at just over 13,000 feet. The air is precious and . . . there is fire in it—that is it, another quality to the eerie atmosphere of the place—it is what shimmers in the air and bounces off of the water. The Sun. It is palpable, as though the air is filled with particulate fire. I try to describe this to Antonio, but he has left me. He walks away, toward the place that he pointed to, and I follow at a distance. He walks slowly and I lag back, as we descend a long gentle grade toward a twenty-foot rise.

Suddenly I am alone. I know it. I feel that Antonio has left me. He is confident that I will follow, so I walk alone, with the stark white pinnacle of Illimani dominating the horizon to my right as my only point of reference, for I am familiar with nothing else here.

"Walk with me to Eden," he had said. "I would like your company on a trip that I must make alone." His words come back to me as I watch him up ahead of me, his ponchos wrapped around the *mesa* slung over his shoulder, his white shirt stained with sweat and dust, an eighty-odd-year-old man climbing a short cliff and disappearing over the edge.

A few minutes later I stand near him, but not with him.

The provenance of the Children of the Sun is a flat, arid, rock-strewn spot in the center of the island. At first glance nothing appears to mark this most sacred place of the Americas—nothing manmade. I look to Antonio and follow his gaze to the formation I had glimpsed at a distance. On closer inspection it is a remarkable thing, a wall of igneous rock, all one piece and convoluted with deep womblike invaginations and hollows formed when it was molten. It makes a sort of semicircle, and I climb on top of it and look down. Its back is smooth and falls all the way down the side of the island, as though a tidal wave of lava washed up onto the island, and as it reached the top, crested, and began to break, it solidified.

I turn and look back down at Antonio. He is facing west—his back is to me; and I see the other thing that designates the spot. There is a stone table here. Thirty yards from the sacred rock sits a solid slab of granite on four granite blocks embedded in the earth. It is an irregular shape but perfectly flat and two feet thick. And there are four more blocks of stone set about the table—they appear to mark the four directions, and they do . . . precisely.

It is one o'clock. I descend from the stone and approach the stone table. Antonio looks up at the Sun.

His voice is distant sounding. "Let us meet here after sunset." He nods a couple of times, then quotes a popular adage of theoretical physics. "If you travel far enough," he says to no one in particular, "you eventually return to the place whence you began."

17

The world was all before them, where to choose
Their place of rest, and Providence their guide:
They hand in hand with wandering steps and slow
Through Eden took their solitary way.

—*John Milton*

July 10

Second morning on the Island of the Sun. Alone, on the beach a few hundred feet below the site of last night's gentle drama.

The Sun has just come up on the other side of the island. In a few minutes it will hit the stone table and eventually illuminate this favorite place of mine—a sandy cove on the west side of the island. But the sky is lightening, there are even a few clouds reflecting the orange sunrise.

Our boat is moored here, fifty feet offshore, its anchor planted on the beach. It waits to take us away from here when we have finished what we have come here to do. Our skipper must have circumnavigated the island and spent the night on board. He poked his head over the cabin top and waved excitedly.

I swam here yesterday, and the water was ice-cold even in the sweltering heat of midday. Perhaps I will brave it again if there is time . . .

I must climb back up the hill soon.

We arrived at the sacred rock and the stone table yesterday at midday, then separated. I came here, Antonio disappeared into the ruins of the rudimentary Temple of the Sun that clings to the western slope about a hundred feet from the stone table. He wanted to be alone. He knows that I know that this is his journey. He has an agenda of his own and knows that I will respect it without question, in spite of my curiosity and suspicions.

So I took a swim and lay on the beach and slept, dreamed, woke up as the Sun was setting in four colors before me. I can't remember the dream.

The darkness of last night was never complete because the moon rose full and shining bright silver an hour after sunset. The place was bathed in silver light.

Antonio had laid out his *mesa* in the east. And he had made four *despachos*—offerings of corn, coca, *pisco,* and *kiwicha* seeds on small squares of tree bark given to him by La Mascadora de la Coca. These were placed at the four directions—ten feet or so behind each of the four stone "chairs" around the table.

As the moon rose, he called on the Four Winds, the Mother Earth, Father Sun, Viracocha. It was a formal invocation with none of the emotion of Sillustani, but of captivating intensity.

And all that we did was meditate. We sat on the stone chairs around the table. Slowly the heat accumulated by the table during the day was released by the stone, and eventually it became cool, then cold.

This was *his* ceremony, and I did nothing but make myself fully present, cleared my mind, and followed his cues.

For the most part, I simply sat there on this island at the top of the world and watched the moon and the stars move across the sky.

Two things happened.

Antonio changed seats a number of times. He would rise and burn a *despacho,* light a match and set it on fire, then return to a different seat. Although his position did not correspond to the specific *despacho,* I could sense that there was some order to it, but I can't explain it.

The strange thing is that more than once in the course of the night—in the bright moonlight—there seemed to be four of us sitting around the table. Sometimes I saw Antonio sitting across from me and sensed two others on either side; and sometimes it was as if I were looking at myself sitting across from me. It was a subtle thing, and fanciful, but worth noting.

And there was something else. I think I tasted synchronicity. There were moments—so simple that I can hardly write about them—when I was overwhelmed with a feeling of accomplishment and gratitude. Times—more than once—when my heart was so filled with thanksgiving that my chest swelled with the feeling and I sighed—and looked up and a star shot across the sky in the place where I looked. I was curious about this, and I spent a long time examining the sky for others. But there were none—no activity in any of the four quadrants. But later, when the feeling was in me and I glanced up, another meteor would burst and streak through the atmosphere. And it happened again, just before we closed the ceremony. If *ayni* can be felt, I believe that I know it now.

The Sun is up. No time for a swim. I must climb back up the island. I hope that my friend is there to meet me.

He is there, sitting on the edge of the table. In spite of the wear and tear and sleepless nights, he looks better than I have seen him in years. He sits smiling and erect, his white *manta* shirt neatly tucked into his travel-worn trousers, his face a few shades darker with all of the sunshine that it has absorbed, and the whites of his eyes and his straight teeth and the silvery hair and grizzled moustache all stand out against the rich, brown-toned skin. The detachment of yesterday is gone without a trace. He is an eighty-odd-year-old man transformed.

He greets me warmly, looks back at me with a fondness that has always been implicit between us.

"Thank you," he says, "for sitting with me last night."

"Thanks for saving me a chair."

He has prepared a breakfast for us. It is laid out with a great deal of care on the eastern chair—the granite block. Cold coca tea, small mounds of toasted *kiwicha* seeds that taste like malt, *quinoa* seeds, bananas, and bright yellow strips of dried honeyed mango that he must have brought all the way from Cuzco.

"Wonderful!" I sit beside him and take a drink of tea. He peels a banana.

"Last night was very important to me. You should understand . . . perhaps you do?"

"No. Tell me."

"For a thousand years men and women have come here before they died. You have seen the terraces here—" he gestures with the fruit—"most are abandoned—but the island once supported the thousands of pilgrims who came to make *ayni*. Now . . . for the last few hundred years . . . it is only the shamans who come, to make *ayni* to the four directions and to discharge the *pacha*—to set free the mooring lines that bind them to the four corners of the world. This is supreme *ayni*, when you give away everything that is yours, when you consciously return your life to the elements without any expectation of reciprocity. And what better place finally to acknowledge your harmony with the four elements than here, where earth, air, fire, and water meet? What better place to celebrate your freedom from them? He breaks the banana in half and hands me a portion.

"The four elements . . ."

"The Medicine Wheel leads to a consciousness of Nature, a harmony . . . an intimate relationship with the elements and with all of creation." He takes a hearty drink of tea.

"So the burning of the *despachos* . . . ?"

"Was the symbolic act to express my gratitude to that which belongs to the Earth."

Now all of my suspicions are realized. Still I am unwilling to accept it. "You did not come here to die," I state flatly. He finishes his banana and starts on the honeyed mango.

"My friend, you know that there are many lives in a single lifetime. It is important to acknowledge when one has ended so that we may begin another . . ."

"Antonio—"

"I have lived for so long in two worlds. Now I am choosing one. Like La Mascadora de la Coca, I will exercise my own invisibility."

"I don't understand."

"Yes, you do," he says. "Because we come from the same source, our genealogy is the same. The psychologist, the shaman, the storyteller—the healer, the magician, and the artist. Our authority comes from experience, not social ordination or faith. We seek the same things. I have studied philosophy and religion and I have explored for myself the territories where they first grew. And I know that from the moment when we first saw our reflection in a forest pond and became aware of our mortality we have been looking for our creator. We have spent the lifetime of our species looking for the creator by examining the creation. But the creator is invisible in the creation. You cannot find the storyteller in the story that he tells—or the composer in the music that he writes. The creator cannot be found by dissecting the creation."

"Invisibility . . ." I begin, not knowing where it will take me.

"And time," he says. "And the ability to keep a secret even from yourself—the lessons of mastery—all of them clues to what we are becoming, what we are beginning to glimpse as we grow. Have you had enough to eat?"

I nod. He scoops up the remaining seeds and blows over them and scatters them all around us and brushes off the top of the stone. Something is going to happen—it feels as though the tension in the air, that shimmering resonance, that crackling tension, is about to snap.

"Lie here," he says. "Take off your shirt and lie on the table. There is something here that I think you should be able to feel . . . better to understand. . . ."

I peel off my shirt and climb up onto the stone, still cool with the night. I lie on the stone table with my head toward the Sun, now 30 degrees above the horizon. Antonio's hands are on my head, his fingers at my temples; he is cradling my head, standing between me and the Sun.

"Breathe," he whispers, and for a long time I lie perfectly still; breathing steadily, deeply from my stomach, I let my muscles go. And still holding my head like an offering to the Sun, he summons to me the powers that he divested last night—his intonation is a whisper, but clearly I hear him summon the spirits of Illimani and of the four *apus*—Ausangate, Salcantay, Huanakauri, and Sacsayhuaman, the "head of the jaguar" of Cuzco.

Then gently he rests my head on the stone and steps away, and the Sun penetrates my eyelids, fills my vision with blood-filtered light, and I continue to breathe the charged thin air, to clear my mind, to give myself to the moment.

"Breathe."

I exhale. Something is happening. The light is changing and I will not interfere with a thought—one thought and the moment will collapse. . . .

The red that filled my field of vision has gone to orange, to yellow. It is filling me. . . .

For a long while I lie here and his words are whispered echoes in the glowing cavity of my head.

He tells me everything. He whispers to me what he knows to be the truth. Until now he has hinted at a secret that we keep even from ourselves; now he tells me what he knows. He plucks away the shroud of mystery that has hidden the simple truth of his being. And whether he is right, or wrong, it is what he believes and I know that, like the Buddhist, he only believes what he knows.

He whispers to me:

"When the Sun shed a tear that landed on the Earth, the Sun gave his children a token of what they would become . . ."

And what started as the sunlight penetrating my eyelids is now a yellow white-hot Sun burning a hole in a blue sky that I look at and then drop my gaze to the sand that my boots sink into with every step.

As Antonio whispers to me I walk, heading east toward a wind-whipped sand ridge whose shape appeals to me. I am not thinking about anything in particular, it is simply that I carry the memory of the Island of the Sun—like any memory, it is resident, there to be summoned, although I am not consciously remembering it as I walk.

My legs are bare and tanned; my thick white socks just clear the top of a new pair of high-top hiking boots—the spaces between the laces are filled with sand. It has been a year since my return from Peru, since I last saw Antonio Morales.

And now his last words are coming back to me. My favorite and most bittersweet memory.

And I know that this must be the moment that I experienced on the stone table when my friend showed me Vilcabamba, when my very being was filled with light and I became, for a moment, invisible. The sand dune is just ahead. I wonder what I will see over its edge. . . .

And then he brought me back. He touched my shoulder, and I opened my eyes and my forehead was tingling and I saw nothing but the sky over Lake Titicaca, felt the hard warm surface of the stone on the back of my head, my shoulder blades, my elbows, the tips of my fingers. I blinked and pushed myself up from the slab, and my head swam, and phosphenes—tiny pinpoints of light—darted crazily before my eyes. I swung my legs over the edge of the table and faced him.

It was astonishing to see him standing there, his head thrust forward slightly, his face contracted with concern. He did not know what I had felt, what I had seen, but it meant everything to him that I felt and saw what he hoped for me, and I knew that I had. I will never forget the expression on his face; simply, I had never seen him anxious before. And while I caught my breath—I suddenly realized that I had stopped breathing, no notion of how long I had been breathless—I managed to sigh out a sort of dazed laugh and he, too, drew his first breath. I needed time, time to sort through what had happened, what I knew was about to happen.

Because I had leapt forward spontaneously to a time when everything that he was about to say to me was a memory.

"Antonio—"

He raised his hand to stop me. In hindsight, I suppose that he had to interrupt. There was more to be said, much more. It took everything that I had, all of my will to concentrate on his words and not the phenomenon that I had experienced, to listen to his words and ignore all that I knew about why we were here.

And then he said something. And rather than break the shimmering silence there between us, it was as though his words were a part of that silence.

18

Everlasting farewells! and again, and yet again
reverberated—everlasting farewells!

—Thomas de Quincey

HE SAID: "IT BEGINS WITH THE CHILDREN."

I stood there, squinting at him in the incomparable brightness of midday on the Island of the Sun. *It begins with the children.* He had said that to me before—five years ago, in the echo chamber behind the Temple of the Spirit Flight in Machu Picchu. There is a room, a rectangular chamber behind the temple, where words whispered at one end can be heard at the other end, even on the other side of the wall, at the dais of the temple. *It begins with the children.*

On that occasion, five years ago, we had been speaking of destiny in low tones that echoed in the chamber, just as they were supposed to. You should not seek to control destiny, he had said. Control of destiny is an oxymoron, a self-contradictory notion. He had said that a person of power could *influence* destiny, learn to dance with it, "lead it across the dance floor of time." And I had asked him where to begin—at the end of our adventures together, I had asked him where to begin.

"With the children," he had said. That was when he tapped the top of his head with his forefinger and said that the crack between the worlds was the fontanel, the gap in the skull that we are born with, that closes soon after birth. Then he had dismissed it all with a wave of his hand and said that we could split atoms and splice genes, that the threads of our destiny are in our hands, that we have the *ability* to lead ourselves into a noble future but we lack the wisdom.

"And it begins with the children?" I had asked.

And he had nodded. And then he had taken my hand and told me that we would meet again, that we had traveled well together, that there were places where he could not go alone.

I stared at him now, standing before me. Bare-chested—he had removed his shirt while I had been on the table—his dark skin darkening in the unfiltered radiation to match the V of deep tan at his throat, his silver-gray hair pushed back from his forehead, the gray pencil mustache under his hooked Quechua nose, the Rasputin eyes with something new in them: something like earnestness.

"You thought that I meant that we must teach the children," he said, quietly responding to my unspoken memory. "That we must nurture them to be nourished by the Earth. You thought that I meant that although the crack between the worlds is here—" he raised his hand and forefinger slightly to suggest the gesture of touching his head—"and that it closes soon after birth, that we must work consciously to keep their spirits open, to see with all of their eyes that they might be able one day to look steadily at the wisdom that has evaded us—that you and I have only glimpsed."

I stared back at him. I almost shielded my eyes from the Sun.

"You thought that it is our responsibility to *teach* that begins with the children. And you were right to think so," he said. "But there is more."

He paused here and swallowed. His head, which was slightly cocked to one side as was his custom when speaking—as though he were observing carefully the effect of each word—straightened, and he looked squarely into my eyes.

"The *lessons* begin with the children, too," he said. "You can only teach truthfully if you find truth. You can only find truth if you seek for it yourself, for the truths of history are the truths of others. Our ability to know truth is changing because we are changing and we must seek truth for ourselves and for our changing species.

"But truth is like a mirage in the desert. For us, the task is not to chase truth but to create it. Truth is a stance, an act of power that you bring to all of your actions. Truth is what the person of knowledge brings to every moment."

He stopped, and his head moved forward ever so slightly; he was expecting me to say something. I was a student again, and there was not much time. That is how it felt: There was not much time. And I knew why. I knew now why the clock seemed to be ticking faster than before. Nevertheless I had to be here, in the moment and fully present *now*. The temptation merely to witness the sequence of a remembered dialogue was powerful. I was still struggling to focus on his words rather than on my memory of a memory that I would have in the future. I wanted to reach out and touch him to make sure that this was real. I am still attached to what is, for lack of a better word, *real*.

I had to forget it—ignore everything that I knew about subsequent questions and answers and events.

"How . . ." I faltered . . . "how do we do it?"

He closed his eyes and nodded with relief. "It begins with the children," he said. "The unborn child who knows nothing of the world, who knows only the world of the womb that surrounds him and protects him and feeds him—if given the choice—might elect to stay there in the perfect comfort, the complete security of what he has known all his life. But the rhythms of Nature push him to make an epic journey, to travel forth into the unknown—the *will* of the mother is to deliver him forth into his next world. Every child begins life as a hero of an epic journey from what is known and secure and comfortable into what is unknown, undefined, even hostile. The unknown is that which we fear the most, that which society and our culture protect us from; yet we begin life by facing it boldly, and then we spend the rest of our lives avoiding it. We make a journey from one womb to another, and we are content to stay there—because we have a choice."

I opened my mouth to say something; I cannot remember what it was, only that he would not wait for my interruption.

"The Earth is our mother. The rhythms of Nature encourage us to go forth boldly, to leave the security of the womb, to face the unknown, and there will we find wisdom. It is a lesson," he said, "and it begins with the children."

I looked at him standing there before me with such utter simplicity, then turned my head away to the great lake that surrounded us. I turned completely, a full circle, and took in the glistening water, the enigmatic islands, the odd shapes of igneous rock floating on a shining sea, the cirrus clouds near the horizon, the shimmering air—looked around as though to remind myself of where I was, standing on the crest of the Island of the Sun among the rubble of dun-colored rock shards and bits of pottery, a blasted barren place, alone with this man, my friend. We might have been the only living things on an odd planet, facing each other at the highest point of a land of rock and water and the light of a sun.

I knew what happened next. Luckily, emotion overwhelmed me, stopped the chaos of reason.

"It is time for you to go," he said.

"What?" He was distorting before my eyes—the whole scene—Antonio and the background of lake and sky wavered in my sight. My eyes were brimming with tears. With my finger, I wiped them away.

He turned away and circled the table, fetching en route his *mesa,* still bound in its cloth with a cord that made a shoulder strap.

"Please," he said, "a favor. . . ."

He handed me the bundle. "Take his back with you to Cuzco. Take a day, and take the train to the *altiplano.* Walk to the hill. As the Sun sets, face each of the four directions, hold the *mesa* up like this and blow sweet oils over it to the south, west, north, and east, blow its life force, its *pacha,* back to the *apus,* to Ausangate, Salcantay, Huanakauri, and Sacsayhuaman. Then bury it in the earth, return it to its place."

I stared at him, comprehending more than the eeriness of a present already remembered. It was my love for this elegant old man. I felt it the way I felt the gratitude that had filled me when I looked to the sky and saw the falling stars.

I said: "And you're asking me to leave you here?"

"The boatman will take you back to Copacabana—"

I repeated my question. He nodded.

It was like repeating a formula, a series of questions and answers that we had repeated before. But that did not make any difference anymore. He said:

"What have I been but a shadow who has followed you everywhere you go? We are thoughts, thoughts that have been given a form. You began this journey back to Peru because of the dreams that you had. Well, I have had dreams, too, my friend. Two nights in April I dreamed that I was with you, walking by your side through the mountains, telling stories of history and legend. And when you were in the jungle, I spent that night in the dream time. I moved by your side and felt your fear. The Campas saw a jaguar by your side—I have always wanted to inhabit such a form, and I did. That very night. But you saw this young boy." He shrugged and looked out over the sparkling water, then back at me. "I do not claim to understand everything that I experience—I am too old to be so foolish—but I can only think that it was I. Perhaps he is what I will become." He exhaled two quick puffs of air, like blowing out a candle. "You know all of this, already, don't you?"

"Yes," I admitted. "It will take some time to sort it out."

"Of course." He looked down at the ground between us, then his eyes strayed to the granite table where we had spent last night, where I had lain just moments ago.

"Perhaps one day," he said, "you will bring your children here. And you will show them where earth and air and fire and water meet, show them the four corners of the world, and become invisible yourself as you tell them the first story ever told."

I took a deep breath, and said: "And you?"

His face smiled at me. "I am going to Vilcabamba."

19

The spirits that follow us are
pursued by us, too.

—*Antonio Morales*

THE DESERT IS A MORTAR, TIME IS A PESTLE, AND life is the grist. Scoop a handful of sand and see there the evidence of the friction of time on particles not quite reduced to their elements. Tiny crystals and bits of ancient forests petrified, shell shards of bygone seas, hooves of primal mammals that wandered gentle plains, microscopic morsels of bone and motes of lava stone, agate and jade and obsidian, a fleck of carbon from a Precambrian fire. Things living and dead, animal, vegetable, mineral, all shifting under a surface of a dun-colored sea where no man dips his oar. A landscape that fascinates as change fascinates, as constancy fascinates, because it is constantly changing. If sacred places are those where the mind and the landscape meet and one describes the other, then surely the desert has always been sacred, a landscape of the soul where anything can be written.

It was February 1991, and I sat on the sand in the middle of the Death Valley dunes.

A year and a half ago I left Antonio standing by the stone table on the Island of the Sun and made my way down to the cove and waded through the knee-high water and boarded our boat and motored back to Copacabana, where there was nothing for me to do but to catch the first bus for Puno.

I had a hell of a time at the border. My *salvoconducto* had gotten wet somehow, and for a while it looked as though I would have to go to La Paz, to the U.S. Embassy, for a new passport so that I could reenter Peru. The Bolivian border guard was easy—I was a Peruvian returning home; I recited my I.D. number from memory and slipped him twenty dollars. But fifty yards away, on the Peruvian side, I wasn't about to pose as a Peruano. When the dust settled, we agreed on a crisp one hundred dollar bill, my soggy *salvoconducto,* and a promise that I would be godfather to the lieutenant's son the next time I passed through—this with a sly grin and a pat on the back and his best wishes for my safe return to the United States.

I got back to Cuzco twenty-four hours later, at six P.M. the next day, ate a light supper and slept until five A.M., then slung the *mesa* over my shoulder and caught the early train for the *altiplano.*

Six months ago I returned to California. Much has happened since then. *The Four Winds: A Shaman's Odyssey into the Amazon,* was published, and much of this book was written.

My wife completed her residency at Stanford University Hospital, and my son turned three.

Three months ago I learned that Ramón's compound was overrun by the Sendero, and the jungle that surrounds it was stripped and burned. So Antonio was right: My last night there (or ours) was not a hallucination, and I had tasted the future then, too.

I continued to lead workshops and to see clients, and twice I conducted seminars in Death Valley. And I had wrestled with my expectations. On both occasions, when the setting was right for me to realize my vision of the Island of the Sun, I had, in spite of my efforts, seen nothing beyond the dunes. How can one know that something will happen and not alter the present in order to affect the anticipated moment? It is the same as knowing what Antonio believed—knowing the vector of our evolution and not allowing that knowledge to divert our intentions or pervert the authenticity of our lives en route—not turning it into a cliché or an apology for being human. That is why it is a secret that we keep, even from ourselves.

Now, the group of friends with whom I had traveled to Death Valley had scattered, and I sat on the sand, baking in the Sun. I took a long drink of water and stood to stretch my back. I was actually thinking about the long drive home at the moment of recognition. The dune had been there, right in front of me, all along—it was the angle of the Sun that had changed, all but imperceptibly. I was aware of my heart—thudding faster. I pointed to the dune; I was alone, but I pointed to it, showed it to myself. Déjà vu, but this time I *knew* where I had seen it before. I suddenly found myself wondering whether or not it is possible to affect the past. We affect the future with every breath, every glance, every moment of our being, but what about the past? The idea that what happens today just might depend on something that happens a year and a half from now. . . . Then I remembered that Antonio had mentioned this in Sillustani, among the tombs of those who had mastered time.

And then I remembered what it was that he had whispered in my ear as I lay on the stone slab of a table on the Island of the Sun.

"When the Sun shed a tear that landed on the Earth, the Sun gave his children a token of what they would become," he had murmured. "Remember that we are the children of the marriage of the Earth and the Sun."

It all came back to me now . . .

"We have spent the lifetime of our species reproducing and mutating and evolving. Survival and reproduction. When we observe Nature in the course of our lives, it seems as though the whole of Nature is a conjugation of the verb *to eat*. Life depends on eating other life, eating and being eaten, the *uruboros*, the serpent eating its own tail . . .

"The unbroken circle of life, the inseparability of life and death, of the life *in* death and death in life. It is not immortality—there is no such thing as this—it is eternity. The circle will remain unbroken. Forever where there is life there will be the death and renewal that life depends on. But we must look further than this, we must see that all the while that we live and die, for all of that time, we are tasting of eternity and we are growing.

"The truth is that Nature is a conjugation of the verb *to grow*. We are on our way. Simply, we began as light from the Sun, and now we—you and I and all our species—have become complex beings, able to think and to reason and to dream, and we are still exercising our muscles, still and for a long time a chrysalis in a state of becoming something new. And around and around the Medicine Wheel we travel; but every time it is different, for we are different. We are growing, changing. Constantly. Do you feel it?

"Do you see what the secret is? The secret that we keep, even from ourselves? We know it for a fact, as you knew the first story ever told, and I knew it, and that young man with whom you walked to Machu Picchu knew it. Breathe deeply—

"We can think, my friend. We can dream with our eyes open. We can travel throughout the universe, free from time and space and the need to understand.

"We can hold a universe inside our minds.

"It is our imagination that must be allowed to evolve, set free, nourished, nurtured, because we of all of the creatures who are Children of the Sun and the Earth can dream, and with imagination we can hold a universe inside our minds. And thought can take form. There are thoughts that give form to matter the way magnets bring order to iron filings on a piece of paper. The universe is a Divine thought that has taken form.

"We can imagine infinity and we can hold a universe inside our minds, and the sacred time is the time when we can give form to our thoughts.

"The secret that we keep, even from ourselves, is that we are becoming gods."

And then he had touched my shoulder and I had opened my eyes to see him standing there anxiously in the sunlight. "And it begins with the children," he had said.

Now, a year and a half later, this was the memory that I carried with me across the sand. The laces of my boots *were* caked with sand, although they were no longer new. . . .

And then I crested the dune, and there before me was the place that I had been drawn to. It was so appropriate a place that I laughed, and the sound of it was snatched from my lips by a warm breeze. If I could have followed it with my eyes, I might have seen the funny shape of that sound bounce and skid along the sand, up the slopes, and down the dunes.

There before me was a crater in the desert, a perfect circle of flat, cracked sand crust veined with salt, surrounded all the way around by high-crested dunes. An arena. I thought: *arena,* Spanish for sand. An *arena*

arena. Theater in the round. I ran down the steep slope, the sand sliding on itself before me in V-shaped waves, my boots leaving dimples on the dune-face. The heat-cracked crust was brittle and crunched underfoot as I walked straight across the circle. Seventy paces, roughly two hundred feet in diameter. I walked the perimeter of the circle and thoughtfully marked off the four directions. From the floor of this basin, my horizon was sand in every direction. My privacy was complete.

So I went to the very center of the circle, the hub of this great medicine wheel I had drawn in the desert, and I sat there for a long time.

I think that Antonio was right. This is the place where gods are grown. Extrapolate our evolution. Chart a course of the growth of human awareness and human potential, and follow the curve past the present and beyond the place where it leaps up, off the edge of the graph. It will rise forever.

I am convinced that the neocortex is the brain of foresight, that our history is the history of the growth and stretching and developing of this muscle of consciousness. And now is the time for humankind to turn the toned muscle of consciousness on itself.

We are alchemists. We can split atoms and splice genes. We can capture the energy of the Sun to fuel our machines. We can feed the world.

But what of our spiritual evolution, the responsibility yet to be grasped?

Around and around the circle of life and death we travel, and every time is different, for we are different, and we have outgrown the old myths that once inspired us to action. The human drama at the dawn of the twenty-first century is not the drama of the last century. The new myths, the stories that will teach our children and endow them with the will to live epic lives, must be forged—lived and told—by us. Nature is a conjugation of the verb *to grow*, and the complacent and apathetic will always be the victims of change. Those who choose their destiny consciously will be the heroes, the pioneers, the midwives, and the mothers of the future.

Antonio was right: the teaching *and* the lessons begin with the children.

Hands clasped, elbows on knees, I sat there at the end of my story, a child myself, and remembered the year when I came to know my father—my fathers: the one whose name I carry, the one who took me by the hand,

and the one who shed a tear that fell upon the Earth. And I imagined a time—ten years from now?—when I will take my son by the hand and we will go to the sea at the top of the world, where earth, air, fire, and water come together.

My heart thudded, marked time. My eyes stung and I sighed with pure pleasure when the tear that I had not shed, the tear that I had wiped away on the Island of the Sun, fell to the hard-baked sand between my legs.